WE DID NOT CARE

HOW THE SEATTLE SEAHAWKS SILENCED ALL DOUBTS AND BECAME CHAMPIONS

CHAMPIONS

This book is available in quantity at special discounts for your group or organization.

For further information, contact:

Triumph Books LLC
814 North Franklin Street
Chicago, Illinois 60610

Phone: (312) 337-0747
www.triumphbooks.com

Printed in U.S.A.
ISBN: 979-8- 89855-008-0

Content packaged by Mojo Media, Inc.
Joe Funk: Editor
Jason Hinman: Creative Director

All photos by AP Images

Contents

INTRODUCTION

FEBRUARY 8, 2026

Whoever said nice guys finish last never met the 2025 Seattle Seahawks. A team defined as much by the integrity and camaraderie in the locker room as by its excellence on the field has reached the pinnacle of the sport, lifting the franchise's second Lombardi Trophy.

Mike Macdonald was the youngest coach in the NFL when he was hired in 2024. He becomes the third-youngest coach to ever win a Super Bowl and is among a select few to do so in his second season. The foundation was set a year ago when he partnered with John Schneider to assemble the pieces for the league's best defense. A champion was built in year two through daring and deft decisions to move on from their starting quarterback and star receiver while signing a derided castoff at quarterback, discarded veterans on the defensive line and at wide receiver, and precocious rookies on the offensive line and in the secondary.

Students will study the brilliance of what John Schneider was able to accomplish in building multiple Super Bowl winners with completely different rosters and coaches. Unlike the first time, this rise to glory was not only unexpected—it was disparaged. Rarely has a team endured so much ridicule, only to prove there are good reasons armchair analysts are not making these decisions.

We witnessed the rise of an Offensive Player of the Year, the redemption tour of Sam Darnold, and the revenge of Cooper Kupp and Ernest Jones IV. Klint Kubiak brought an offensive system and a cohesive coaching staff that started the year with a historically explosive passing attack and finished it with one of the league's best run games.

One of the youngest rosters in the league is set up to find sustained success, even as Kubiak exits to take on his own head-coaching opportunity. The "Dark Side" defense embraced life in the "Death Zone." Jaxon Smith-Njigba dunked on goalposts and "fan" defensive backs in San Francisco. Grey Zabel pounded Busch Lights and opposing defensive linemen. Nick Emmanwori sacked quarterbacks and blanketed their receivers.

Players were bound by a creed: Mission Over Bullshit (M.O.B.). That was tested in a troubling opening-season home loss to the 49ers and in a four-turnover loss to the Rams. They responded with a win over the Steelers on the road after the first setback, and Jones set the tone by speaking up for his quarterback after the loss in LA. The team would not lose another game after his message was delivered.

Their path was a healing one. It took them to San Francisco to secure the top seed in the conference, followed by two home games that reignited a legendary home-field advantage over their two biggest rivals, before finally hoisting the trophy on the 49ers' home field. They beat the MVP and the MVP runner-up.

There can be no question that this Seahawks team was the best in the NFL. However, that is only part of their story. Macdonald captured their essence with a fiery four-word soliloquy when asked about the doubters: "We did not care."

This is the story of the men who shaped this team and brought glory back to the Pacific Northwest. ■

Mike Macdonald (right) enjoys the postgame celebration alongside running back Ken Walker III. Walker was named Super Bowl MVP, the first running back to take home the award since Denver's Terrell Davis in 1997-98.

SUPER BOWL LX
FEBRUARY 8
2026
VINCE LOMBARDI
TROPHY
NFL

SUPER

SUPER BOWL LX
SEAHAWKS 29, PATRIOTS 13
February 8, 2026 • Santa Clara, California

NO DOUBT ABOUT IT!

SEAHAWKS THROTTLE PATRIOTS, LIFT LOMBARDI FOR SECOND TIME IN FRANCHISE HISTORY

Perfection is often a mirage.

People chase it in their appearance, their careers, their relationships. It forever evades them. They think they have what they want until they see someone else with more or better.

True perfection usually is fleeting. It is the sunset with a loved one, your child's first laugh, a first kiss. Football makes this a harsh reality for fans who loyally follow their teams. Each play, each quarter, each game presents an opportunity for joy, only to regularly turn into despair or envy. A win streak can snap. A rival can outshine you.

There have been 50 seasons of Seahawks football. Forty-eight of them of ended with a loss. Not this one. The Miami Dolphins may claim the only undefeated season, but your 2025 Seahawks just finished a perfect season of their own. The script they wrote was so full of goodness, Hollywood would have rejected it due to unbelievability. Believe it. The Seahawks are Super Bowl champions once again, and oh how sweet it is.

Forget who plays for this team, who coaches them, or who works in the front office. We will get to them in a second. Think about what would have been the dream scenario for a Seahawks fan before this season.

Start with a team that is ridiculed. Create that underdog tale the Northwest loves. Add in a vicious defense that strikes fear in opponents. Now weave in a playoff path that involves maximizing 49ers and Rams misery. Beat the 49ers on their home field to secure the top seed. Beat them again on your reinvigorated home field. Make it a humiliating loss for good measure. Welcome in a cocky Rams team that does not respect you, and beat them and their MVP quarterback for the second time in three games. Take a trip back down to your new home-away-from-home in Santa Clara and beat the team responsible for the most scarring loss not only in franchise history, but maybe in sports history. Do it on your rival's home field. Deck out their stadium with your green and blue colors. Hang massive pictures of your players inside and out. Lift the Lombardi Trophy surrounded by confetti and drench each other in champagne in their home locker room.

Come on.

That is so silly that no Seahawks fan would have dared to even imagine it. Now add in the people.

Sam Darnold is a Super Bowl Champion. The same guy who was the butt of every joke and dismissed throughout this season no matter how many games his team won or how much evidence he provided. He may still see ghosts, but they will be the haunted souls of all the people who said he would never be here. He finished the playoffs with no turnovers despite facing Rams and Patriots defenses that excelled at making life miserable for quarterbacks.

Sam Darnold, Ken Walker III, and Mike Macdonald hoist the Lombardi Trophy together after the Seahawks defeated the Patriots at Levi's Stadium in Santa Clara.

NFL

88

Cooper Kupp and Ernest Jones IV were tossed aside by the Rams.

Kupp is one of the world's great people. He is humble and kind and hard-working and incredibly talented. He gives more than he takes and has a fantastic sense of humor. The Rams discarding him was understandable, but they took it an extra step and snickered at him for fumbling in the first half of the second Rams game. Chris Partridge, the Seahawks outside linebackers coach, almost came to blows with Rams coaches for the slight. Look who's laughing now.

Jones was anointed the new leader of the Rams defense by Aaron Donald after he retired. Sean McVay and Les Snead decided they knew better and traded him for a bag of chips before last season to the lowly Tennessee Titans. How fitting for him to find his way to the Seahawks.

In fact, the Rams were a primary reason Darnold became available to sign in Seattle after they sacked him nine times in the playoffs last season. That combined with their Kupp and Jones decisions contributed greatly to their own demise as all three played big roles not only in the wins over LA, but across the whole season.

Opposite: Confetti falls as the Seattle Seahawks celebrate on the field after winning Super Bowl LX. Above: Mike Macdonald laughs after getting doused by his players.

Linebacker Derick Hall (58) had two of the six sacks on New England's Drake Maye, who was out of sorts much of the game due to Seattle's defensive pressure.

MOSES
76
71
90

SEAHAWKS
61
SEAHAWKS
9
26

Who they are as people was as important as who they were on the field as players. Darnold's otherworldly ability to flush bad plays or bad games rubbed off on his teammates. But it was Jones' fiery defense of his quarterback after he was in peril that will be remembered as the final stitch in the tapestry of this championship squad.

"Sam's been balling," he told reporters after Darnold's four interceptions against the Rams in Week 11. "If we want to try to define Sam by this game, Sam's had us in every f–king game. So, for him to sit there and say, 'That's my fault,' no it's not. It was plays that defensively we could have made, opportunities where we could have got better stops. It's football, man. He's our quarterback. We've got his back, and if you've got anything to say, quite frankly, f–k you."

Seattle never lost again. Be sure to thank the next Rams fan you see for gifting Seattle Darnold, Jones, and Kupp. That is, if you can find one.

Mike Macdonald becomes a Super Bowl winner in just his second season at the helm. He told anyone who would listen that he expected to win it all throughout the offseason. Most took it as typical coach speech. He meant it. People will talk about him for his savant play calling, but his biggest contribution to this team might have been his willingness to admit he needed help growing as a leader.

His work with performance psychologist Michael Gervais helped him bring his vision of a connected locker room to life. They instituted walk and talks, mixed up the locker room assignments, leaned on Neiko Thorpe's penchant for fun to launch shadow boxing competitions that spread like wildfire, forging bonds that will last a lifetime.

This team played not to prove other wrong, but to lift the brothers they loved.

The Patriots felt like an afterthought. We could recount the plays that led to the 29-13 win, but that would be like focusing on the flower instead of appreciating the Spring that nurtured the seed.

Ken Walker III rushed for 135 yards on 27 carries while also catching two passes. Walker's 135 rushing yards were the most the Patriots defense allowed all season.

C
USA
250

Macdonald constantly preaches process over results. The process this season was a work of art. Each day was maximized. The team never got high or low. They managed a steady burn that led to the league's best point differential and three losses by a combined nine points.

They only trailed by 10 points or more twice all season. They won one of those games and had a kick as time expired that would have won the other.

Coaches like McVay and Kyle Shanahan scoff at special teams. Macdonald hired Jay Harbaugh to torture the league. No team had more return touchdowns. No kicker has ever scored more points. No punter has merited consideration for Super Bowl MVP until this one.

There were no weaknesses.

This team could run. They could pass. They could defend the run, rush the passer, cover. They scored when they kicked off. They scored when you kicked off. There was nowhere to hide. No quarter was given.

So much can be traced back to the defensive line that was built in every possible way by John Schneider.

Opposite: Defensive tackle Rylie Mills takes down Drake Maye for a sack. The six Seattle sacks were tied for the fifth most in Super Bowl history. Above: Cornerback Devon Witherspoon (21) dislodges the ball from Drake Maye, which was caught in the air by teammate Uchenna Nwosu (7) and returned for a touchdown.

BARNER
88

He traded for Leonard Williams. He drafted Byron Murphy, Derick Hall, and Boye Mafe. He signed Jarran Reed, DeMarcus Lawrence, and Uchenna Nwosu as free agents.

What was an embarrassment just two years ago when the Pittsburgh Steelers rolled into town and ran them over with the playoffs on the line became the most feared position group in football. It was fitting that Hall had two sacks, including the back-breaking strip sack in the Super Bowl. He and Mafe played selflessly all year where so many young players would abandon their brothers in the name of a flash play that would get them a bigger payday down the line.

That happens because guys like Williams, Nwosu, Lawrence, and Reed set the standard and held people to it.

If Williams and crew were the muscle, Devon Witherspoon was the heart. His infectious energy was on full display as he became a human blur on the way to sacking Drake Maye once and causing the game-ending fumbleception that Nwosu returned for a touchdown.

There are not words that can describe the respect he commands in that locker room. He is about ball and lifting his brothers. There is nobody quite like him.

The defense came together for form The Dark Side. Nothing so dark has ever created something so bright.

It would be hard to talk about what made this team special without talking about the offensive line. A source of misery for over a decade, this group became one of the most promising young units in the NFL.

Grey Zabel became an instant starter and looks to be a future All-Pro. Charles Cross stepped into a leadership role in his fourth season. Abe Lucas finally had a chance to play healthy. Jalen Sundell got to play next to former college roommate and ended the season as one of the more promising centers in the league. Anthony Bradford rebounded from rough moments to contribute heavily to the run game. They will be a group that can be the foundation for years to come. Teams with great offensive lines always have a chance.

Tight end AJ Barner catches a touchdown in the fourth quarter to help give the Seahawks a commanding 19-0 lead.

SEAHAWKS
USA 250
7
50

None of this happens without John Schneider. He made all the right moves, starting with hiring Macdonald. No GM has ever won two Super Bowls with two different coaches and two totally different rosters. Until now. This ring cements him as one of the best in the history of the sport.

Perfect seasons don't come around very often. We may never replicate the satisfaction that comes with this win and this season. Chasing perfection misses the point. What happened this year is permanent. It is written in ink. We started this season thinking perfection was a mirage, but as the confetti falls, it looks pretty real to me.

This is ours. Forever. ■

Opposite: Linebacker Uchenna Nwosu celebrates his pick-six of Drake Maye, which effectively put away New England in the 29-13 Seattle win. Above: Super Bowl MVP Ken Walker III was taking it all in following the second Super Bowl win in franchise history.

ROAD TO THE SUPER BOWL

JONES
71
KENNEDY
96
12
80
45
SEAHAWKS
The Trusted Network for AI
BECU
LUMEN
aws
DELTA
It's better over here
210
212
DELTA SKY360° CLUB
SEA
NFL

LEAP OF FAITH

JOHN SCHNEIDER STICKS NECK OUT, TRADES GENO SMITH

MARCH 8, 2025

The goodbye was tearful.

Pete Carroll spoke of his wife, Glena, and his voice cracked as he displayed a rare moment absent of joy and optimism. An era was ending in Seattle. The best era. One that saw them reach heights that still offer delight upon reflection many years later. Carroll spoke about the opportunity in front of his former partner, John Schneider, to lead the franchise. The fact that Schneider remained when Carroll did not indicated ownership believed the talent on the team was superior to the results the coaches were producing.

There was some validation in that belief when the defense that had been spiraling downward for a decade, rose to nearly a top ten unit and the team won 10 games in the first season sans Carroll. There were still vestiges, though, of the culture and talent that Carroll had cultivated underpinning the success of this new staff. Geno Smith's revival in the NFL was a product of his talent fusing with the confidence Carroll imbued and the opportunity presented.

While many fans felt Smith represented a ceiling for how good this team could be, he was more of a floor raiser than a ceiling setter. This offseason was always going to be tightrope walk for Schneider. His trade of Smith to the Las Vegas Raiders removes the net.

CARROLL SHADOW LOOMS

Attachments to players tend to be more pronounced in coaches than personnel departments. Coaches are working with guys more often and in close quarters. General managers and scouts are constantly looking for new faces who have the potential to be better than players already on the roster. Getting too attached to a player is almost antithetical to their job. Carroll and Schneider were in perfect alignment when they first arrived in Seattle Carroll had not yet formed any attachment to players and Schneider was free to explore every avenue to improve the team. That quickly changed as the pair built a championship roster in record time. Carroll was a steadfast proponent of many of the players and coaches that lifted the first Lombardi Trophy in Seattle. Schneider saw the inevitable effects of age and injury. Fissures began to appear what had been a shared vision between Carroll and Schneider.

Releasing an injured Richard Sherman, saying goodbye to Bobby Wagner, pursuing a trade of Russell Wilson, were all decisions that were reported to come from Schneider's desk. Carroll, of course, had veto power and could have overruled. In fact, he was reported to have done exactly that when Schneider had agreed to the framework of a trade for Wilson to the Chicago Bears a full year prior to when the quarterback was ultimately moved. Part of Carroll's superpower to create a fully bought in and motivated locker room comes from his loyalty to the players. It also appeared to blind him at times to the decline or flaws in players and coaches.

Schneider almost certainly looked at Smith's age (will turn 35 this season), price (rumored to be $40-45M per

President of football operations and general manager John Schneider began the offseason makeover of the Seahawks with the trade of veteran quarterback Geno Smith to the Raiders.

year), and production, and set a hard limit on how far he would go to keep him in Seattle. Carroll is the last person to see age as a barrier to production and wants a player he knows and loves to create a winning culture right away.

Sam Darnold is the favorite to become the next Seahawks quarterback, according to multiple reports. His asking price is expected to be lower than Smith's. Assume for a second that his contract will be between $30-37M per year, and that it will include performance escalators he has to meet that protect Seattle from his breakout season being an aberration.

That would mean Schneider saw two options in front of him:

OPTION 1

- Sign Smith (34, turning 35) at $40-45M per year for 3 years.

OPTION 2

- Sign Darnold (27 years old) at $30-37M per year for 3 years
- Add a 3rd round pick

Despite the fact that Darnold outperformed Smith statistically in 2024, Smith is widely considered the better quarterback. There is some proof of that perception in the fact that a team like the Raiders chose to surrender a 3rd round pick and reportedly plan to extend Smith instead of simply signing Darnold themselves.

Option 2 seems appealing on face value, but it comes with far more risk. Darnold is just a few years removed from joining the Carolina Panthers as a starter and throwing only 9 TDs in 11 starts while tossing 13 interceptions. If Darnold was the product of a terrific offensive coaching staff in Minnesota last year, along with arguably the best receiving corps in the NFL, Seattle could find themselves falling out of mediocrity instead of rising above it.

This decision puts a ton of pressure on his second-year head coach and their brand new offensive coordinator, who touted Smith as a major reason he was excited to be here. This doesn't even account for the potential of a DK Metcalf trade.

What even the most ardent Smith supporters need to acknowledge is that his time as the Seahawks starter was coming to an end at some point in the next 2-3 years, barring a trip to the Fountain of Youth. Some may point at the long career of a guy like Tom Brady as evidence that Smith had more in the tank. The reality is that last year was mostly a referendum on older QBs.

Kirk Cousins (35), was signed to a big deal and now may be released. Aaron Rodgers (41) was mediocre and unable to lift the Jets. Russell Wilson (35) had a brief flash and then plummeted to the point of possibly losing any chance of being a starter again in the NFL. Even Matt Stafford (37) regressed massively during the regular season before salvaging his job with a terrific set of playoff performances.

Schneider has to know there is more risk in the path he has picked. Darnold, at his best, is a similar player to Smith at a younger age. Signing him would have no effect on their desire to draft a young heir apparent. It may increase the odds that they consider using their first pick on that position.

The best way to mitigate this risk is to have a proven veteran in Darnold compete with a rookie and a guy like Sam Howell to see who earns the starting job. That is nothing new to Schneider who once signed Matt Flynn the same year he drafted Russell Wilson and already had Tarvaris Jackson on the roster.

It would be ideal if that rookie was picked after the first round to alleviate the pressure to play someone taken that high. The question for Schneider will be whether he believes the guy he likes will fall to them in the second or third round as Wilson did. That is where a Metcalf trade could come in, either netting a second first round pick or, more likely, a high second. Owning a pick in the 30s could give Schneider some confidence that he could get one of the QB prospects he likes.

IMPACT ON METCALF DEAL

One of the more fascinating aspects of this upheaval is the interplay between the Metcalf and Smith situations. All signs pointed to the Seahawks wanting to sign both players as recently as a week ago. There were reports of teams inquiring about Metcalf, but that is very different than the team wanting to trade him.

Reports indicate there was meeting with Metcalf that ultimately led to the receiver requesting a trade. That trade request was made public Wednesday. Reports say that Smith was offered a deal that he declined, and no counteroffer was made. As of this morning, Jordan Schultz reported that Smith requested a trade the day after Metcalf made that request.

Was the Smith request related to the Metcalf request? He had made no secret of his love for having a player like Metcalf as a target. Maybe the combination of another new offensive coordinator without either Tyler Lockett or Metcalf in the receiving room was enough to make Smith prefer to go elsewhere.

There is also the possibility that Metcalf's trade request came after he had some indication that the Seahawks were going to be making a QB switch. His side has mentioned wanting, "quarterback stability," as part of their reason for requesting a trade. That could have been a reference to the older Smith being replaced by a younger player over the course of Metcalf's next deal or this churn we are witnessing right now.

Maybe most intriguing is the potential that Metcalf was not enamored with Smith as the quarterback here and part of the reason he wanted out was to play with someone else. If that is the case (and there are no credible reports that it is), the trade of Smith might open the door to Metcalf signing an extension with the Seahawks after all.

Darnold did pretty well with Justin Jefferson and Jordan Addison last season. Perhaps that is part of the pitch to Metcalf. Should Metcalf still want out, the Raiders may no longer be a potential destination if he has doubts about playing with Smith.

One of the most striking aspects of this situation is that it appears the team wanted to keep both players. Metcalf has forced their hand by going public with his trade request, and then Smith did the same, albeit privately.

Mike Macdonald has not been here long enough or forged deep enough relationships to help bridge gaps between the front office and these players. You could imagine someone like Carroll intervening to bring the two sides together. While a laudable skill, that may not always be in the best interest of the team. Holding on too tight to players who either do not want to be there or are later in their careers is not a great recipe for creating an ascending roster.

The upside of all the risk the Seahawks would be staring in the face if both Smith and Metcalf are dealt is that they would have the opportunity to create a young core that would not be limited by age or price tag. Imagine if Smith stayed and played splendidly this season. You still would need his replacement within a few years. There is no such limit now.

MORE TWISTS REMAIN

As much as it seems Darnold is the team's top choice, there is the chance he signs elsewhere. Things get pretty dicey if he does. Rodgers is a name that has come up given his prior relationship with Schneider in Green Bay. That would be an unmitigated disaster. A fanbase that was already split on Smith would almost universally despise Rodgers on a variety of levels. His only redeeming quality would be the knowledge that he would only play a single season before yielding to a younger option.

Justin Fields is said to be headed back to Pittsburgh, but Seattle could change that equation. Fields is young (26), has game-breaking running ability, and some connection with Jaxson Smith-Njigba from his time at Ohio State. Fields is also a pretty awful passer, who has not done well in play-action or under-center, which are staples of the Kubiak system.

Cousins could be an option, but his lack of mobility following his injury makes him a challenging fit as well. Jimmy Garoppolo was an option for the Rams if they moved on from Stafford and might be an option here. Derek Carr, who was Kubiak's quarterback in New Orleans, might be attainable given the Saints cap situation. Schneider has always been enamored with Drew Lock. Zach Wilson could convince someone to give him another shot. Trey Lance is a free agent for the first time. If these names send shivers down your spine, keep that in mind when you reflect on the Geno Smith era.

One name you will not hear is Wilson. Multiple reports have confirmed he will not be considered. That bridge is pretty burned.

NATIONAL FOOTBALL CONFERENCE
CHAMPIONS
NFL

We also heard that Schneider initially tried to pry edge rusher Maxx Crosby from the Raiders in exchange for both Smith and Metcalf. Las Vegas declined and soon extended Crosby, but that indicates Seattle could be in the market for another pass rusher.

Myles Garrett is the big name. Trey Hendrickson of the Bengals was recently given permission to seek a trade. Both players are around 30 years old, which a buyer beware time for pass rushers, but keep an eye on whether Seattle wades into those waters.

SLEIGHT OF HAND MEETS SLEDGE HAMMER

The fan base has been apathetic the past few years, especially last year. Their favorite players had mostly gone. Their beloved coach was gone. Their replacements neither had the charisma nor the results on the field to generate new enthusiasm and engagement. Trading Smith has woken a hornet's nest of activity and interest. Some are crestfallen and furious. Some are energized and optimistic. Many are curious.

Seattle has more cap space than almost any team in the NFL, even before trading Metcalf or restructuring Uchenna Nwosu's deal. They have no excuse to be outbid on the open market for a player that can make them better. Fans would be more excited to hear Schneider had signed center Drew Dalman than to hear they got a new quarterback.

If he goes after bargain basement offensive linemen and signs a journeyman quarterback in Darnold and then reaches for a quarterback in the first round, this could be the beginning of the end for his time in Seattle. If he adds one or two quality free agent linemen and drafts another, while getting a Day 2 rookie QB to pair with a younger version of Smith for cheaper, the Seahawks history books will remember him very differently.

Do not turn around and sign one of the aging veteran receivers. Do not bring in a toxic presence like Rodgers. Do not deviate from your best player available draft strategy that has worked well the past three years.

Schneider has to exit a Metcalf trade with at least a high second round pick, and likely more, to have a good shot at coming out of this better in a year or two. Seattle currently has four picks in the Top 100. A Metcalf trade could give them six. That is the kind of ammunition that could infuse your roster with young talent at a variety of positions and allow the new coaching staff to build the identity they seek. This can be the start of something new and special.

All this prestidigitation has captured the attention of fans and the league. That will quickly fade if Seattle does not emerge from this cloud of construction as a much tougher and more entertaining team. ■

John Schneider's vision of replacing Geno Smith with Sam Darnold paid off in a big way.

49ERS 17, SEAHAWKS 13
September 7, 2025 • Seattle, Washington

STARTING WITH A THUD

SEAHAWKS MAKE SKEPTICS LOOK LIKE PROPHETS IN SEASON OPENING LOSS

Week one of the NFL season is misleading.

The first Seahawks Super Bowl team in 2005 got walloped by the Jacksonville Jaguars to start that year. The first Seahawks team to win a ring needed a miraculous late touchdown pass to Jermaine Kearse to escape the Carolina Panthers, 12-7. Neither game was a good measure of the quality of those squads. It would be a mistake, though, to wave away the concerns that resurfaced in this consequential 17-13 loss to rival San Francisco. Part of the hope building for this team during preseason was the idea that old narratives would be challenged, and outside skeptics would look foolish. Instead, this performance reinforced most the flaws that have been raised about this team's construction and added a few more.

The nuts and bolts of this game were pretty simple. Seattle's offense was anemic. The 49ers offense was not much better (5.3 yards per play versus 4.6 for Seattle). Brock Purdy was the better quarterback and Kyle Shanahan was the better offensive play caller. That especially showed up on 3rd downs where the 49ers converted 50% of their tries (7-14), compared to 30% (3-10) for the Seahawks, including the game-winning touchdown. There have been years when Seahawks fans would have taken a moral victory out of having clearly closed the gap with the bully 49er crew. There were simply too many familiar flaws that left most frustrated, and some smugly wagging their "told you so" finger.

Consider some key points of disagreement entering this season.

THE OPTIMISTS

The belief was that Mike Macdonald had finally found his offensive counterpart in Klint Kubiak and that the offense would commit to the run in a way they never did last season. The young offensive line would be worlds better than any of the recent products due to health, talent, experienced coaching, and scheme. Ken Walker III and Zach Charbonnet would form a powerful and explosive due who would run behind battering ram fullback Robbie Ouzts and quality group of blocking tight ends and receivers.

There would be plentiful under center snaps with play action that made runs and passes indistinguishable. The receiving room would be talented enough to take on a supporting role behind the run game for occasional chunk plays with some veteran presence in Cooper Kupp who could make some key 3rd down and red zone plays. Tory Horton Jr. and Elijah Arroyo would burst onto the scene as productive rookies. Sam Darnold would run the offense efficiently and cut down on some of his sacks by getting rid of the ball more quickly.

Linebacker Ernest Jones IV (13) and the Seattle defense limited Christian McCaffrey to only 69 yards on the ground, but it wasn't enough in the 17-13 loss to San Francisco.

SEAHAWKS
13
SEAHAWKS
MCCAFFREY
23

The defense would take a step forward in their second season under Macdonald, with more players joining Leonard Williams as dominant playmakers. DeMarcus Lawrence would help a first down weakness from last year and be a still-productive run defender while the other young edge players in Boye Mafe and Derick Hall would take their next step as pass rushers. Byron Murphy II would emerge as a more disruptive presence in the middle of the line. Nick Emmanwori would allow Macdonald to play a larger nickel package and deploy Devon Witherspoon in new ways.

Macdonald's resume of giving NFC West offenses trouble would become a possible division-altering storyline.

THE PESSIMISTS

Seattle downgraded at quarterback and wide receiver and brought in a mediocre offensive coordinator who will not be able to lift a team without playmakers. The offensive line will still be one of the worst in football. Opponents will stack the box to take away the run and dare Darnold and a subpar receiving room to beat them. Only JSN will be a weapon in the passing game. Kupp is washed and Horton is a 5th round rookie. The tight ends are nothing special. Darnold will shrink under pressure and in the big moments.

The defense will be good, but not great. Edge rush will be a problem and Murphy won't be much more than he was a season ago. Emmanwori will struggle as a rookie. Riq Woolen will continue to make key mistakes. There may also be some issues at inside linebacker outside of Ernest Jones IV.

Macdonald will do a good job coaching the defense but still does not have a good offensive philosophy, and the team will be too limited on that side of the ball to be a quality playoff performer.

EARLY EVIDENCE

The Seahawks run game was the most important aspect of this football team heading into the season. I have said repeatedly that they need to be a Top 10 rushing offense to be a good team. The one aspect of that projection that seemed safe was that Seattle would commit to the run after suffering through Ryan Grubb's pass-happy play calling a year ago. In some ways, that proved absolutely true. Seattle had the second-highest early down run rate in the NFL (pending MNF).

In other ways, it felt like a departure from the under-center, wide zone, play action, identity they practiced and preached all offseason. Seattle ranked 19th in the NFL in run outside the tackles (50%), per Next Gen Stats. More alarmingly, they were dead last in play action rate (4.2%), with just a single recorded play action pass attempt. That one attempt was a 21-yard completion, leaving Seattle with the second-highest EPA per dropback on play action passes in the league.

Their quick passing game was horribly ineffective. Kubiak dialed up screen passes that seemed more likely to lose yards than gain them. In fact, Seattle is currently dead last in the NFL in EPA/DB on quick passes (under 2.5 seconds) at -0.73. You can read that as Seattle lost nearly a point per play (estimated) when running quick passes. That problem gets worse when you realize quick passes made up 54% of their pass attempts.

The 49ers run defense was awful last year. The personnel changes they made to their interior line were limited to rookies. Robert Saleh, however, showed why he is considered one of the best defensive coaches out there by outclassing Kubiak all day. His ability to limit the effectiveness of the run game, while suffocating the quick game, left Kubiak grasping at straws.

It was bizarre to see Kubiak get away from the under-center game as much as he did. It wasn't until the penultimate drive to take the lead that they truly committed to that style. On that drive, they had runs of 8, 5, 7, and 4 yards before having a -1-yard carry. They did not see a 3rd down until they had already moved into field goal range. Where was this the rest of the game?

Macdonald talks about wanting to "throw their fastballs," by which he means doing what they do best. It felt like they were messing around with secondary pitches all day and wound up losing a game where they did not honor their intended identity on offense.

Walker had a particularly unproductive day that will only increase the calls for Charbonnet to take over the bulk of the carries.

There are some odd takes out there that this game proved Darnold was a fraud last season and using this game as a chance to relitigate the decision to move on from Geno Smith. That conversation will continue all season (and maybe beyond) but feels like wasted breath.

Darnold was actually a wildly different quarterback in this game than he was a season ago. His time to pass was 2.59 seconds, 8th-fastest in the NFL so far. That number was 3.08 seconds last season, 3rd-slowest in the league. As previously mentioned, his shotgun rate was higher, and his play action rate was way lower.

One commonality between last season and this one was that Darnold remained a productive deep passer. He ranks 9th in EPA/DB on throws over 20 yards. The problem is that he had just two attempts.

He seemed on the precipice of continuing another trend from last season where he was the top-rated passer in close and late situations until the fateful fumble that lost the game. He finished with zero turnover-worthy throws, per PFF.

Generally, this game felt far more like an indictment on the Kubiak game plan and play calling than it did on Darnold.

The offensive line played reasonably well. When not blitzed, the Seahawks had the 3rd-best pressure rate in the league (17.6%). You might think that is completely related to the quick passing game, but they were still 15th in the NFL on pass plays that took over 2.5 seconds. Where they struggled was when the 49ers blitzed.

Seattle gave up pressure on 71.4% of pass attempts when Saleh called a blitz. That was the 5th-worst rate in the league. Overall, they wind up in the middle of the pack (16th) in pressure rate after this game.

Run blocking was probably a little better than it looked given how many players the 49ers were committing to the run. Seattle averaged 1.15 yards before contact, 16th in the league. They did that against stacked boxes on nearly a quarter of their rush attempts (23.1%).

Nick Bosa was a handful, as always, but only had two pressures on the day. Unfortunately, one of them winds up counting as a sack as he drove Abe Lucas back close enough to Darnold to cause the ball to slip out of the quarterback's hands.

The bigger factors were guys like Kalia Davis and Jordan Elliott, who were far more stout in the middle than expected.

Overall, the offense was about what you would expect from a new coordinator, quarterback, and receiving room in the first game of the year. The hope was that they would burst onto the scene as a surprise group, led by a dominant run game. That did not happen. Most of the credit there goes to Saleh, but some of the blame certainly goes to Kubiak.

Defensively, the group looked a lot like they did over the last half of 2024. They were sound and tough. Purdy was under pressure on over 60% of his dropbacks, which was a career-high and ranks tops in the NFL so far. The 49ers struggled with the blitz even more than the Seahawks, giving up a league-worst 83.3% pressure rate when Macdonald blitzed.

Coverage was mostly excellent, allowing the 3rd-lowest average separation (2.9 yards) in the NFL. The problems, though, were all too familiar.

Riq Woolen was in position to be the hero twice on the game-winning drive for San Francisco. Twice, he was the goat. Purdy had already thrown two interceptions when he lofted a pass to Ricky Pearsall down the left sideline. Woolen was in great position to pick off another pass but misjudged the ball and allowed Pearsall to separate and make the biggest gain of the day. Later, Purdy threw up a desperation pass to little-used tight end Jake Tonges that should have been, at worst, knocked down by Woolen. Instead, Woolen did not attack the ball and Tonges surged in front of him to catch the game-winner.

This happened to Woolen against the Rams last year. It happened against the Vikings. He has the talent to be one of the best corners in the game but failing to make the play in the biggest moments will limit his value.

The loss of Emmanwori early to an ankle sprain forced Ty Okada into the lineup and he was badly outplayed in his six snaps. So much so that he never returned to the field. It was clear Emmanwori was a big part of the game plan against the 49ers, and Macdonald had to adjust in real time.

That he still limited Shanahan to 17 points for the second-straight game, and his players were able to pick off two more passes, is encouraging. Murphy was more disruptive in this game, if not dominant. His win rate on true pass sets (16.7%) was similar to what he did last year (20.7%), while getting more chances. He had 13 snaps in those situations in this game, which would work out to 221 over a season. He had just 85 of those chances last year. If he can have a win rate that high while his volume of opportunities rises, he may still become the weapon the fans and teams envision.

The edge rush felt too much like last year. Nobody was getting quick pressures, and sacks were hard to come by. Purdy extended plays and found success just often enough to win the game.

Josh Jobe was terrific. Jones was terrific. Williams won the matchup with Trent Williams. Julian Love was great. Overall, this performance should have been enough to win. At the same time, it still felt like a defense made up of quality players but lacking in truly dominant playmakers.

WITHERSPOON
21
EATTLE
NFL
OAKLEY
SEAHAWKS

ROUGH WAY TO START

Chalk up one for the pessimists. Seattle was unable to beat a weakened 49ers team who also lost key players in George Kittle and Jauan Jennings during the game. They controlled a lot of the game but could not convert in key moments on either side of the ball. Losing this divisional game at home will absolutely haunt this team later in the season, just as the Rams loss at home did a season ago.

One thought that came up after this one was that while the 2022 draft class was stacked with impactful players in Charles Cross, Walker, Mafe, Woolen, Lucas and Coby Bryant, there is some question about whether that group can the core of a contending team. This 2025 class feels different in terms of makeup. Somewhere between optimism and pessimism is the idea that this group might be where the team needs to build around, which will take more time than one season. How much they step forward over the course of this year will reveal how quickly they can take on that responsibility.

Seattle has what may be an even tougher matchup this coming week at Pittsburgh, a team with better personnel on the front seven than San Francisco. The book is now out on this offense. Stack the box and stop the run. Double Smith-Njigba and dare Darnold to beat you anywhere else. As Macdonald says, the best way to the other side is through, not around.

That will involve holding true to their under center, play action, identity. This was not the disastrous game we have seen against the 49ers in the past. It also was not the encouraging step forward Seahawks fans were hoping to see. A surprise win on the road would go a long way toward getting back on track. ■

The Seahawks gave their doubters plenty of ammunition in the disappointing Week 1 loss to the division rival 49ers.

SEAHAWKS 31, STEELERS 17
September 14, 2025 • Pittsburgh, Pennsylvania

TRUTH BE TOLD

SEAHAWKS GET KARMIC PAYBACK WITH 31-17 WIN OVER STEELERS

Week one is a known liar in the NFL. The Seahawks are hoping week two is the truth.

Just a few days removed from a gut punch home loss to the rival 49ers, Mike Macdonald and his team flew across the country and put on a performance in Pittsburgh that would make Mike Holmgren and Matt Hasselbeck smile. Known as the Stealers by many Seahawks fan for their controversial Super Bowl victory to end the 2005 season, the Steel City has rarely been a hospitable place for Seattle or any visiting teams. Since the year 2000, just three teams have won more games at home than the Steelers (140). The Seahawks had played just four times in Pittsburgh over the last 25 years and had lost three. Seattle had been shutout only four times in 30 years, and two of them came in Pittsburgh. It was looking like things may go the home team's way again when a series of Seahawks mistakes helped lift the Steelers to a 14-7 halftime lead despite only gaining 69 yards. All three phases clicked in the second half as they outscored Pittsburgh 24-3 to close the game and left DK Metcalf, Aaron Rodgers and Steelers fans exiting Acrisure Stadium empty handed.

This was a game that did not equal the conference and divisional matchup against the 49ers in terms of seeding and possible tiebreakers. It did, however, go a long way toward flushing that loss from their system. Seattle was a larger underdog in this game, and were playing without Devon Witherspoon. The Steelers were flying high after putting up 34 points on the road with their ancient quarterback tossing four touchdowns. Riq Woolen had been admonished by coaches, and Tyrice Knight was at risk of losing his job to Drake Thomas. Klint Kubiak had befuddled everyone with his game plan. Ken Walker III looked like he may no longer be the starter in the backfield. Cooper Kupp looked washed. Tory Horton Jr. was invisible. Sam Darnold and Abe Lucas had a forgettable end to the game.

What a difference a week makes.

Kubiak and Darnold had the Seattle offense cooking from the start in this one. They scored the Seahawks first opening drive TD since 2023, a span of 23 games. The drive included first down conversions on 3rd and 6 and 3rd and 10 to Jaxon Smith-Njigba, and was capped by a 21-yard touchdown pass to Horton on a play action pass from under center. It was also the first catch of Horton's NFL career.

That would be the only points for Seattle in the half. A missed 36-yard field goal by Jason Meyers, two interceptions by Darnold, and a missed interception by substitute nickel corner, Derion Kendrick, turned what should have been a comfortable halftime lead into a deficit.

The most egregious error in the half may have been Kubiak's decision to eschew the tush push with A.J. Barner

Sam Darnold and Seattle's offense looked much better in Week 2, dropping 31 points and 395 total yards on Pittsburgh.

SEAHAWKS
14

that had worked both times it had been used this season, and decide to go with a slow developing play action pass that was blown up by Cam Heyward, and resulting in an interception that nearly cost Seattle the game.

This felt like the worst type of overthinking by the coaching staff. The whole point of implementing a play like the tush push is to have a reliable solution for short yardage situations. The play had succeeded against the stout 49ers front and the Steelers earlier. Why go away from it?

To then call a pass play made the decision even more bewildering. That's the kind of play call that makes sense when you have earned the reputation of a hard-nosed running team that a defense has to sell out to stop in short yardage. Seattle has not even proven that to themselves, let alone opponents.

There was another poor coaching decision later in the game when the Seahawks had a 3rd and 10 at their own 20-yard line. Macdonald called a timeout with the play clock about to hit zero. The chances of conversion there were low, and burning a timeout there was pointless. It came back to burn them when they had a far more consequential 3rd and 6 in Steelers territory with time again running low on the play clock. They did not call for time there and the offense rushed to get off the snap, only to have Darnold throw to nobody as the players were not on the same page.

These are self-inflicted wounds that are simple process fixes. The Eagles don't have to think about what they want to do on 4th and 1. Seattle shouldn't either, until opponents give them a reason to do so.

Fortunately, the team made enough plays with the Steelers making some errors of their own, to dominate the second half.

Seattle scored a touchdown on their first possession of the second half on a drive that was a shining example of the team they want to be. Walker gashed the Steelers for runs of 9, 15, and a pair of 5 yarders. The ball was spread around to three different targets, none of which were Smith-Njigba. The young tight ends got involved with Elijah Arroyo making a catch and Barner punctuating the drive with a touchdown. They were under center for 6 of the 9 plays, with play action utilized effectively. Darnold was 4-4 on the four passes, mixed nicely with the five running plays.

Barner continues to be a red zone weapon. He now has five touchdown catches in his short career, which matches the total from his entire 45-game college career. It also now puts him in a tie with Brock Bowers for most TD catches by a TE in the 2024 draft class. Bowers has been targeted 161 times. Barner has been targeted 43 times.

Kupp was a factor throughout the day. Not only did he finish with seven catches and 90 yards, but 42 of the yards came after the catch. The whispers were becoming shouts that he was no longer a viable NFL receiver. This performance shouted back.

All of this was made possible by an offensive line that took another step forward. Gone were the artificially quick passes that made up over half the throws by Darnold a week earlier. There were longer developing play action passes and straight dropbacks, and the line provided solid protection on the day. A few blitzes got home, but the Seahawks pass protection of the previous decade had trouble blocking 3-4 defenders, so this was still a noticeable improvement.

Abe Lucas appeared to have a particularly strong game, especially in run blocking. Charles Cross had one of the best blocks of the day on a nondescript 5-yard run that had him drive-blocking his man onto his back seven yards downfield. Robbie Ouzts made his presence felt, getting a ton of snaps, often lined up as a tight end. He had a gorgeous pancake block to help spring Walker on his longest run of the day.

Zach Charbonnet and Walker did their best Freaky Friday rendition as they switched places in what seems to be an arrangement where only one back can be productive during a game. Watch out if the Seahawks can actually get both of these guys cooking at the same time.

Walker was finally back to his explosive self. This is a guy who has run behind such bad blocking, it was hard to remember just how good he was as a rookie. He was arguably the most dangerous offensive weapon on the field for Seattle, which is how it should look if things are going well.

This is a player who should be good for a 100+ scrimmage yards every single week. He is too talented and too dangerous to be the afterthought he had started to become. It was fitting that he put an exclamation point on the game by taking a toss play to the left on 3rd and goal from the 19-yard line and ran it in for a touchdown. He becomes the first player in NFL history to score a touchdown on a run of 19+ yards on 3rd or 4th and goal.

He is capable of more. So is this running game.

The man who has earned The Most Dangerous Weapon moniker on this offense is Smith-Njigba. The Steelers came into this game knowing he was the focal point of the pass game. They were going to bracket him all day and try to put their best corner, Jalen Ramsey, on him whenever possible. Smith-Njigba hardly seemed to notice as he ho-hummed his way to another 100 yards receiving. He is quickly establishing himself as not only a viable #1 receiver, but as one of the best receivers in the game.

People said he would struggle without DK Metcalf drawing coverage. They said he was just a slot receiver. They said he wasn't a downfield threat. That chorus of doubters is looking like Rosie O'Donnell singing the national anthem.

Smith-Njigba is beating all comers, all coverages, on all parts of the field. His 43-yard catch on Ramsey's head led to Walker's historic touchdown scamper. Defenses are going to dedicate more and more attention to Smith-Njigba, which only matters if the rest receiving weapons are capable of exploiting their advantages. Kupp, Horton, Arroyo, and Barner did that perfectly in this game.

It felt like Kubiak took the training wheels off Darnold and the offensive line this week. You could feel the trust build as Darnold converted multiple 3rd and long passes. The interception he threw early was a nice play by Ramsey, and not a terrible throw or decision. It was aggressive and risky, but not poorly thrown or to the wrong receiver.

Generally, Darnold looked like a guy capable of carrying a heavier load than most expected him to in this offense. Evidence is mounting that John Schneider may have done the unthinkable and found a quality starting quarterback at a discount in free agency. That simply does not happen in this league.

Darnold still has his weak spots, like sensing the pass rush and turning the ball over too often, but his ratio of positive-to-negative plays has skewed heavily toward the good side over his last 20 games. At some point, we stop waiting for the "Old Sam" to return. Those who would point to his two interceptions as reason to pump the brakes should tally up all the other plays in this game and then look at his process throughout. This was a second straight quality start from the Seattle signal caller.

This Seahawks defense came into the season with far higher expectations than the offense. They played their hearts out against the 49ers and were understandably demoralized by the way things ended. The question was whether they could play with the same physicality and energy a week later without their emotional leader.

Witherspoon made the trip to Pittsburgh and went through an extensive pre-game workout, but he was still not able to run full speed without some hitch in his gate. That meant a new DK had to take over for Seattle, Derion Kendrick. The corner who Seattle claimed off waivers from the Rams, had played almost exclusively outside corner in his career, but had started cross-training at nickel last season before he tore his ACL. The Rams played him some at nickel during preseason, which is probably part of what attracted Seattle to him

He very nearly had more interceptions in this game than Witherspoon has in his career. Rodgers threw a pass right to Kendrick in the first half, which Kendrick not only did not catch, but volleyed up in the air and almost into the hands of a Steelers receiver. He more than made up for it when he made a diving catch of a ball that caromed off the hands of a Steelers receiver in the endzone for a game-changing pick.

Macdonald used a variety of combinations in the secondary to make up for the absences of Witherspoon and Nick Emmanwori. Kendrick played nickel. D'Anthony Bell played big nickel. Ty Okada sometimes came in to play deep safety and Julian Love would walk down to the box.

Meanwhile, Woolen and Josh Jobe were locking down the outside all day. No Steelers wide receiver had more than 22 yards, and all 22 of those yards to Calvin Austin came when the game was out of reach near the two-minute warning. Metcalf was mostly silent. He had his customary drops but did make a rare contested catch in the red zone for the Steelers only touchdown.

Jobe is becoming a big story in this season. Often cited as the weak spot in the secondary, all he has done through two games is play nearly flawless football. Should this continue, his addition will go down as another big win for Schneider.

Woolen could have sulked after a rough week but played with great effort and result. He had one penalty but was otherwise blanketing his opponents on the day.

The biggest story on that side of the ball may have been the play of second year defensive tackle Byron Murphy II, who had a better rookie season than his numbers indicated. His first game this year followed a similar script in that his level of play was much higher than his stats. No need for advanced metrics in this one. Murphy finished with 1.5 sacks and five pressures.

The last time a Seahawks DT has had 1.5+ sacks in a game while playing in the first 15 games of their career was Jordan Hill back in 2014. Disruptive defensive tackles are a rare breed. Ones who have the desire to play both the run and the talent to rush the passer are even more hard to find. This was a building block performance for Murphy.

When Ernest Jones IV heard me mention the multiple sack performance to Tyrice Knight in the celebratory post-game locker room, Jones leapt up from his seat wearing just a towel and said, "Murph got two sacks!! Where you at Murph!?" He then walked off to find him with a big smile on his face.

The linebackers had plenty to smile about themselves. Knight had a big bounce back game that had him flying all over the field making tackles. He acknowledged afterwards that there was some rust after missing 30 days due to injury during training camp.

Special teams deserves a shout in this one. George Holani will get well earned praise for his touchdown recovery of a kickoff that allowed the Seahawks to create some breathing room, but Jason Meyers and Jay Harbaugh should get some shine as well.

Meyers kick was expertly skipped into the landing zone and over the head of the returner. It would have been an uncomfortable catch either way. Instead, the rookie returner made a huge mistake and let the ball settle in the end zone while Holani raced down the field to recover it while managing to stay inbounds.

Meyers also made a 54-yard field goal after missing a 36-yarder earlier. Horton had a nice punt return and Michael Dickson had a good day punting. Coverage was solid all afternoon. The special teams have made big plays in each of the first two games.

In all, the Seahawks won for the third straight time as road underdogs and are 4-1 in those situations under Macdonald. A lot of the disparity in record between home and road can be attributed to quality of opponent. Not this time. Winning in Pittsburgh during their home opener with the talent they have should not be dismissed.

It is also worth noting that the Seahawks opponent seemed to struggle with the physicality of Seattle for the second straight week. A laundry list of Steelers left the game due to injury after the 49ers experienced the same fate.

The laws of physics would tell you that when two objects collide, the object with greater density and velocity will do the most damage. Seattle has felt like the bigger, faster, stronger team through two weeks, even if their record is just 1-1. It has been a long time since you could say that about a Seahawks team facing the 49ers and Steelers.

Just like last week, however, this was just one game. It won't make up for the Super Bowl loss all those years ago or the home opening defeat to San Francisco, but it will allow this team to exhale and start building the belief that they are who they thought they were, and not who the naysayers have said they will be.

Week one is a liar. Seattle hopes the truth will set them free. ■

Wide receiver Cooper Kupp had a quiet debut with the Seahawks in Week 1 with only 15 yards receiving but bounced back with nine catches for 90 yards in the win over the Steelers.

SEAHAWKS
SEAHAWKS
10

SEAHAWKS 23, CARDINALS 20

September 25, 2025 • Glendale, Arizona

A DESERT ESCAPE

SEATTLE SNEAKS BY ARIZONA WITH THIRD STRAIGHT WIN

Seattle opened this season with a crushing loss to the rival 49ers at home. They not only lost, but they did so impersonating another team on offense.

There was one play action pass attempt. They operated mostly out of shotgun. Sam Darnold was given an ultra-conservative game plan that had him throwing most of his passes instantly to receivers and backs who were behind the line of scrimmage.

Mike Macdonald was seething after the game, and the whole week that followed. They wanted to win at home. They wanted to beat a division opponent. Mostly, they wanted to play their brand of football. That frustration led to immediate changes. Seattle went from 4% of their passes being play action to 24% the next week. They went from 60% shotgun to 60% under center. That has remained consistent in the weeks that followed (23% play action, 57% under center). The results? Seattle has the 6th-best offense in the NFL over that span by EPA per play, and the 3rd-best passing offense. They have won three straight. And Mike Macdonald is moonwalking in locker rooms where music blasts and players dance.

Winning football games is hard. You can win with talent, coaching, or luck. What you can't do is win by cosplaying some other team identity. Seattle experienced that last season when Ryan Grubb went rogue and the Seahawks coaching staff was not in alignment. The locker room was not in complete alignment, either. You have no chance of sustained success if you are not at least working together toward a shared vision. There still may be more talented teams or better game plans or rough matchups that lead to a loss. This Seattle team should never lose again by being an anathema to themselves.

This game started so well. Seattle controlled the Cardinals on offense and put together some beautiful drives against a stout Arizona defense. The domination was so complete that even when they were forcing turnovers on their own players, it still felt like a win was certain.

A bad holding call on what should have been a game-sealing touchdown, combined with a tiring defense, and a missed field goal, turned a laugher into a nail-biter.

The Cardinals made big plays against both Devon Witherspoon and Riq Woolen to pull even. It was perhaps fitting that an error by the home team opened the door to a game-winning drive orchestrated by Darnold, Kubiak, and Jaxon Smith-Njigba. Jason Meyers made a kick from almost the same distance he had already missed from, and some combination of elation and relief filled the hearts of every Seahawks fan, player, and coach.

Seattle is now 3-1, with a road division win, and a mini-bye week where they get to rest this weekend ahead

Linebacker Derick Hall and the Seattle defense forced two turnovers and limited Arizona to just 253 total yards in the win.

SEAHAWKS
58
58
SEAHAWKS
50
58

of their big home game against the Tampa Bay Bucs, who will play a physical game against the Eagles this weekend before flying across the country to face the Seahawks.

This was not the game to frame. The Seahawks forced a fumble on their own player after an interception. They got a taunting penalty that cost them points. They blew a big lead. They missed a field goal. They dropped another interception.

Ask the 2016 Seahawks if they would have taken a flawed victory instead of their 6-6 tie in Arizona. Ask the 2024 Seahawks if they would have taken an ugly win over the Rams last year when they had multiple red zone turnovers, a missed extra point, and other mistakes. Ask the Cardinals if they would have apologized for stealing that game.

You take every win.

Doing it on the road, on a short week, against a division foe who was desperate to avoid falling to 0-2 in the NFC West, makes this a game where style points matter less.

What does matter is that Seattle looked like the far superior team on both sides of the ball for most of the game. The Seahawks put up more yards against the Cardinals defense than any opponent this season. They held Arizona to their fewest yards on the year. They sacked Kyler Murray six times against an offense line that came into the game ranked as the 2nd-best pass protection group in the NFL. They rushed for 155 yards against a run defense that ranked 4th in rushing yards allowed before this game. They converted 46% of their 3rd downs against a team that had been ranked 3rd in 3rd down defense. They converted 2 of 3 red zone chances (and should have been 3 of 3) against the 4th-best red zone defense.

They did enough. For now.

The game Seattle played Thursday night won't beat a team with a better quarterback, better coaching, and better weapons. That team is coming to town next Sunday.

Closing football games is an art, and the Seahawks have shown promise on offense and some concerning signs on defense.

Twice, the Seahawks have possessed the football either tied or trailing late in the game. Twice, Darnold and the offense moved the ball into position to win the game. Yes, the first game ended with a fumble, but the drive to get there was noteworthy given Darnold led the entire NFL in passer rating in close and late situations (within 8 points and less than 5 mins remaining) last season. He looks comfortable and courageous in those moments. His offense looks the same way.

This young offensive line has some struggles. They also are showing poise and promise. We have not seen the killer holding call or false start. The pass protection has been mostly quite good even though defenses know they can attack the passer in those situations. Kubiak has dialed up good plays and Jaxson Smith-Njigba has been a velvet dagger. Nobody is killing people as smoothly and silently as JSN this season.

That this offense is operating so efficiently without the benefit of a reliable run game is encouraging and not something I expected.

The Seahawks are 25th in EPA/rush and 22nd in rushing success rate. Yet, they are averaging 32.6 points per game the last three weeks. That is happening because this is one of the best early down passing offenses in football. Seattle is 5th in the NFL in converted early downs (1st and 2nd down) into first downs, doing it 23.7% of the time. They are 4th in EPA/dropback and success rate on early down passes. That rises to 3rd-best if you toss out the anomalous Week 1 game plan.

That early down success is happening because they are forcing teams into run heavy personnel packages with either a fullback or two tight ends, and then exploiting mismatches. They are the most explosive passing offense in football. No receiver has more 16+ yard receptions than JSN (10).

They have also started to add some explosive rushes to the mix. Only Derrick Henry has more 20+ yard rushes on the year (4) than Ken Walker III (3). Walker, though, also has a 20+ yard reception, which pulls him into a tie with Henry for most explosive plays by a running back so far this year.

It will take time for the run game to become more efficient. It may not happen. I'm betting it will. Adding a quality run game to this passing attack could raise this offense into a Top 10 unit that can give any defense headaches. That's the mission, and not one many thought was a realistic goal before the season began.

Defensively, they have been steady and stout in every game. Their mission is to become a group that can close out a game.

That requires having players who rise to the occasion and make impact plays at the moment of truth. Too often, those have gone the wrong way. Woolen and With-

Kicker Jason Myers celebrates after hitting a 52-yard field goal as time expired to clinch the 23-20 win over the Cardinals.

erspoon both gave up plays that could have lost the game. It is understandable that many are going to want to see Woolen benched. That might happen. Derion Kendrick sitting on the sidelines had to get Macdonald's attention.

I will not be writing off Woolen. He remains the most talented corner on this roster, and in the league. He is clearly struggling with confidence in playing the football. This team will be better if the coaching staff can help him with that versus giving up on him.

The pass rush also has to get home in these situations and Macdonald has to dial up the correct pressures and plays. This is a defense full of good players. A key aspect of becoming great is finding guys who will finish games.

Seattle now has an extended break to rest and recuperate. Nick Emmanwori should be set to return when practice resumes. Ailing Abe Lucas and Anthony Bradford could benefit from some time to heal. We will find out about DeMarcus Lawrence and others. It will also give time for the coaching staff to self-scout and make some adjustments. We may notice steps forward in the run game and some new wrinkles on both sides of the ball.

All possibilities remain open for this team because they won this game. Now, we see if they can transform from good-to-great. Meaningful football is back on the menu in Seattle. ■

BUCCANEERS 38, SEAHAWKS 35

October 5, 2025 • Seattle, Washington

FAILING GRADE

SEAHAWKS SHOW LITTLE RESISTANCE TO BUCS, FALL IN SHOOTOUT

Seattle was undefeated when they rolled into Detroit last season with the top-ranked defense in football. They were going to be missing a bunch of starters on that side of the ball, but the hope was that Mike Macdonald would be able to create some sort of game plan to compensate. Instead, the Lions scored 21 points in the first half, 42 for the game, and Jared Goff didn't throw an incompletion on the night.

The Seahawks were 3-1 headed into a Sunday showdown with the Tampa Bay Bucs. They were again the top-ranked defense in the NFL and were without some key members of their defense. The result was achingly familiar. The Bucs scored 38 points and Baker Mayfield set a record by throwing for 379 yards with only four incompletions. Seattle had similar games last year against the Bills and Packers. A team that prides itself on defense has had a disturbing trend of not only playing poorly against top competition but putting up almost no resistance. The result was failing another chance to prove they are worthy of higher aspirations than simply making the playoffs.

Injuries are a big part of any NFL season. Seahawks fans have seen two Super Bowl teams, 2005 and 2014, experience the impact of losing key defensive players and having no way to compensate. Even great teams have limits on what they can overcome. The rough part for the Seahawks in this game was you could point the finger at the players or the coaches and both would be valid.

Seattle entered the game without starters Julian Love, Devon Witherspoon, and DeMarcus Lawrence. The coaches chose to keep cornerback Shaquill Griffin on the practice squad and have Nehemiah Pritchett active. They also chose to have edge Connor O'Toole active and Jared Ivey inactive. Pritchett was called into action when Tariq Woolen left with a concussion in the 3rd quarter. He surrendered more touchdowns (two) in two quarters than Woolen has allowed all season (one). Ty Okada, who was subbing for Love, struggled mightily himself. Derion Kendrick, who had been excellent in two games at nickel corner, also had a rough afternoon.

Macdonald had been able to hide the absence of Witherspoon against the Steelers and Saints because the front four was able to create pressure and he could deploy extra men in zone coverage behind it. The plan was to bring more pressure from different players in this game, while still playing zone coverage. Baker Mayfield and the Bucs hardly noticed there was a defense on the field.

Receivers were wide open. There was only one sack and two QB hits. Running the ball was ineffective, but it hardly mattered when you could average a first down (11.5 yards) on every pass attempt.

To be clear, Mayfield is playing as well as any quar-

Wide receiver Jaxon Smith-Njigba had another big game with eight catches for 132 yards and a touchdown, but it wasn't enough to top Tampa Bay.

WINFIELD JR
31

terback in the league. He is having an NFL caliber season. This is a good offense and may wind up being the league's best when they get back to full weaponry. It is not shocking that they were able to score some points. It is meaningful, however, that the Seahawks were unable to provide any resistance.

Macdonald took responsibility after the game. He undoubtedly was disappointed in how some of his players performed but chose not to point any fingers in public. It was hard, though, to watch the number of players who were open, the degree to which they were open, and the total lack of pressure on the quarterback, and not feel like the game plan and adjustments were a big part of the problem.

Macdonald, for all his impressive moments against great signal callers in Baltimore, still did have some games where he was dominated thoroughly. Mike McDaniel, Sean McVay, and Ben Johnson have all outcoached him at times. His inability to find some adjustment to at least provide resistance in those games is something to monitor. He is still young and does not have the deepest well of experience to draw from. McVay was humbled earlier in his career by Vic Fangio and Bill Belichick. He nearly retired but has come out stronger on the other side.

Macdonald is building a team built around strong defense. He needs that to show up in these big moments against top competition, or this is all just meaningless mediocrity.

Losing Derick Hall was big. It was bizarre that he went down, and the edge player they had active, O'Toole, did not play a snap. Why was he active? Mike Morris took a lot of edge snaps and was not particularly effective. Jared Ivey is a player who seems to bring a better combination of pass rush and run defense on the edge. We will see if the team makes a change there as Lawrence is probably unlikely to play against this week.

Woolen going down exposed just how much worse things can be at corner and may have forced the team to hold onto him the rest of this season. Trading him and relying on Josh Jobe, Kendrick, Griffin, and Pritchett feels untenable. Jobe was not great in this game, either.

A sneaky way to improve coverage and overall defensive stability would be to upgrade the inside linebacker role opposite Ernest Jones. Plug in a Demario Davis or Jordyn Brooks there and the middle of the field would be harder to access for opponents. Tyrice Knight and Drake Thomas are not cutting it yet.

There are some overreactions out there about Macdonald and the defense being exposed and the team being doomed. That is either emotional or uninformed. Mayfield is playing at a level most are incapable of reaching. The defense will get guys back and be a Top 10 unit. The question is whether they can be a true foundational defense that can slow down even the best offenses when it matters most. That question is valid and will remain so until they show up differently in these games.

Sam Darnold and Klint Kubiak almost overcame the bad defensive showing with a sparkling performance against a quality Bucs defense. Kubiak deviated from his early down tendencies. He utilized shotgun the most he has since Week 1 and had an early down pass rate of over 50%. That was middle of the pack in the NFL this week but is notable given the Seahawks have had the 2nd-lowest early down pass rate in the NFL before this week.

The Bucs were the best run defense in football coming into this game. Kubiak decided he could lean on his quarterback and the passing game to soften things up for the running attack. It worked.

Darnold looked every bit Mayfield's equal. He threw for 341 yards and 4 touchdowns, while only having six incompletions on the day. The running game was highly effective as well. Seattle put up 122 yards rushing and averaged over 6 yards per tote, against a team who had not allowed 100 yards rushing all season, even though they faced the Eagles.

They were explosive and efficient and varied. It was beautiful game on that side of the ball.

This was the second straight week of featuring heavy use of two tight ends with FB Robbie Ouzts on injured reserve. Seattle has been the best two tight end offense in the NFL this year, and that continued in this game.

A.J. Barner came into the NFL with a reputation as a blocking tight end with limited value as a receiver. He caught two touchdowns in this game and has team-leading four on the season. He has eight touchdowns since entering the league last year, which is more than the far more heralded Brock Bowers (five). His hands have been terrific, 14 catches in 16 targets, and his ability to impact the game as a blocker and receiver makes him one of the more valuable young players on this roster.

Seattle ranks 1st in the NFL in EPA per rush and 2nd in EPA per pass when playing with two tight ends. They run the ball 50.5% of the time and pass the ball 49.5% of the time. This is their bread-and-butter.

The fact that the offense could perform that well against a defense that had limited their last three opponents to fewer than 270 yards, including the Eagles (200 yards), is reason for optimism.

Being able to win a football game with different aspects of your team makes winning more consistent. Seattle has won games with special teams. They have won games with defense. They nearly won this game with offense.

It was fair to wonder if this offense had been propped up by playing some inferior defenses. The Bucs were the start of a stretch against tough defenses. Playing their best game against that group bodes well.

As great as Darnold and Ken Walker and Jaxon Smith-Njigba were, the offensive line deserves some recognition. The right side, in particular, seemed to open up some holes in the run game. Darnold was not sacked on the day and only was hit twice.

Unfortunately, one of those hits came on his last pass that bounced off a defender's helmet and hung in the air for a game-deciding interception. If you had asked every Bucs and Seahawks fan watching that game what they expected on that final drive, they would have told you Seattle was going to move into scoring position and take the lead. Seattle had scored touchdowns on five straight drives, including a 99-yard beauty that gave them a late 35-28 lead.

Dareke Young had a terrific game, contributing on kick coverage, kick returns, and as a receiver. He is earning a larger role. Jake Bobo had a couple damaging holding penalties he would like back.

The officials played their normal role with some questionable calls. Jason Myers missed another field goal. The crux of this game, though, came down to a defense that couldn't get off the field and an offense that has failed twice at home to complete the game-winning drive. As bad as the defense was, Seattle still wins this game if the offense finishes the job.

The Seahawks have now lost two important home games against NFC opponents. Those will definitely come back to haunt them should they earn a spot in the postseason. Nothing gets easier next week in a trip to Jacksonville, where the Jaguars feature one of the best defenses in football and Seattle may not get significantly healthier. The next test awaits this coaching staff and this locker room. We will find out if the connection they have worked so hard to develop can handle the adversity. ■

SEAHAWKS 20, JAGUARS 12

October 12, 2025 • Jacksonville, Florida

THE BOUNCE BACK

SAM DARNOLD AND SEAHAWKS POLISH RESUME, DOWN JAGUARS 20-12

The morning started with Justin Fields authoring one of the worst quarterback performances you will ever see.

The former 11th overall completed just 9 of 17 passes for 45 yards. He was also sacked nine times for -55 yards, meaning his team finished the game with -10 yards passing. The last time that happened was 1998 when Ryan Leaf went 1 for 15 with just four yards passing as the San Diego Chargers finished with -19 yards passing.

After Fields finished, another former top pick threw for nearly 300 yards, two touchdowns, and helped his team improve to 4-2 on the season. That same Sam Darnold who is forcing his way into the MVP conversation, is just two years removed from a Fields-like game himself, where he went 5 for 15 for 43 yards and two interceptions for the Carolina Panthers. It was just last season that he threw zero touchdowns and three interceptions against the Jaguars in Jacksonville. Fields can take some solace in the redemption story Darnold is writing with each throw. Only one quarterback has won more games than Darnold's 18 since the start of the 2024 season (Jared Goff, 19). Baker Mayfield helped his old teammate by beating the 49ers and ensuring the Seahawks would end the day tied for first in the NFC West.

The story of this game was not really about Darnold or the Seahawks offense. It was about the relentless Seahawks pass rush that registered a staggering 17 quarterback hits, the most that a Seattle defense has recorded in the last 25 years (and maybe longer, since the data only goes back that far). Trevor Lawrence was the town bike. Byron Murphy II sacked him on the very first play. DeMarcus Lawrence and Uchenna Nwosu sacked him on the Jaguars last play. In between, he was pressured on more than half his dropbacks and sacked a total of seven times.

Jacksonville was riding high after beating the 49ers on the road and the Chiefs at home on Monday Night Football. There was some talk that Liam Coen's offense would be able to exploit the same holes his former team, the Bucs, exposed in the Seahawks loss last week. Those analysts failed to realize the distance between Lawrence and Mayfield is roughly the same as the Seahawks flew to arrive in Florida.

Lawrence had trouble identifying and escaping pressure. He made a number of off-target throws and his receivers did not help him out. The only production came from blown coverages by the Seahawks or circus throws while running for his life. Seattle silenced the Jags running game, as they have done to every team this season.

The Seahawks allowed over 5.1 yards per rush and 0.0 EPA/rush when in light boxes last year. They are at 3.6 yards per rush and -0.24 EPA/rush this season. This matters because it is allowing Mike Macdonald to deploy more players in coverage without sacrificing his ability to take away the run.

Being able to count on the guys upfront to both stop the run and rush the passer has allowed Seattle to weather the storm of injuries in the secondary where Devon Witherspoon has played just one healthy game and Julian Love has missed a number as well.

Running back Zach Charbonnet and the Seahawks improved to 4-2 with the tough road win at Jacksonville.

JAGUARS
41
26
NFL

Macdonald knew he would need a better pass rushing performance than the team put up against the Bucs to cover up the absences. Interestingly, that did not mean a higher rate of blitzing. The Seahawks only blitzed 14% of the time, which was below their season average.

What they did appear to do was incorporate a creative rush plan that had interior players like Leonard Williams and Murphy lined up outside as edge players, with typical edge players like Lawrence and Nwosu and Boye Mafe lined up inside. They ran a lot of games and stunts out of these formations that confused and overwhelmed a Jaguars offensive line that had allowed just 6 sacks and the 2nd-lowest pressure rate coming into the game.

Macdonald and Aden Durde have mentioned multiple times that Nwosu is one of their best game-runners. There is timing and instinct required to excel in that type of rush, as opposed to just winning off the edge with an array of pass rush moves. Nwosu is proving his coaches right with 4.0 sacks in the last three games. Only Nik Bonitto and Tuli Tuipulotu (5.0 sacks) have more over that time.

Seattle managed all this mayhem without Derick Hall and with Mafe producing no sacks or QB hits. The Seahawks have not had three defensive linemen finish with 1.5+ sacks since the 2012 Fail Mary win over the Packers.

This was partially about game plan, and largely about the guys upfront taking over the football game. There was some friendly debate and competition during training camp about which part of the defense was the "tip of the spear" between the secondary, the linebackers, and the defensive line. That debate has largely been settled. This defensive line is not only leading the defense, they are setting the tone on the entire team.

Leonard Williams, Jarran Reed, and DeMarcus Lawrence are all veterans who are also excellent players. That is proving critical for a young team. Their impact goes beyond their play on the field. Young offensive linemen like Grey Zabel are asking them for advice on a daily basis. When there were tensions during a physical 1v1 pass rush drill in camp, it was Williams who always insisted the offensive and defensive linemen always gathered together before the drill was over to reinforce that they are part of the same whole.

Their physicality is leaving opponents battered. Their quality and coaching have helped the Seahawks offensive line outperform expectations. This season's ceiling will be set by how dominant that group can be.

One issue for the team has been closing out games on both sides of the ball. It was starting to look like that might bite them again after the Jags scored a touchdown to make it a one-score game with most of the 4th quarter left to play.

The offense responded with a 3-and-out drive that netted -1 yards. The defense, however, stopped the Jaguars on three straight drives that totaled 12 plays and 17 yards. The most impressive was the final drive when Jacksonville took over at their own 36-yard line with 4:03 to go in the game and all their timeouts.

This was a clear four-down series, where the Jags would go for it the whole way. Rookie Nick Emmanwori sniffed out a screen pass to Travis Hunter for a loss of a yard on first down. Ernest Jones broke up a short pass on second down. Tank Lawrence and Nwosu teamed for a back-breaking sack on third down that made it 4th and 18. Coen had no choice but to punt.

That gave the Seahawks offense one more chance to do their part. This time, they did. On 1st and 10 from their own 27-yard line with 2:53 to go in the game, Klint Kubiak dialed up his best play call of the day. The Jaguars were expecting a run that would force them to burn one of their timeouts. Kubiak gave them a run look from under center but called a play action pass where tight end AJ Barner crossed the field away from the direction of the expected rushing attempt. Darnold lofted a ball deep down the field that settled into his young tight end's hands for what would turn into a 61-yard play that effectively ended the game.

It was not a clean game on offense. Kubiak and Darnold have been much better in other games this season. That said, the Jaguars entered the game with one of the best defenses in the league by some measures, and Seattle managed to be the first team to exit a game against them without turning the ball over.

They also were explosive. The play to Barner was the capper, but the dynamic between Darnold and Jaxon Smith-Njigba continued to be must-see TV. The third-year receiver is looking like the best receiver in the game. He is on pace for close to a 2,000-yard season, which would clear the franchise record by a ridiculous 700 yards.

He is playing with the grace of a gazelle, the speed of a cheetah, and the grip of an eagle. Nature had something special in mind when assembling his particular set of skills. He was the fastest player in football in Week 6, reaching a top speed of 21.1 MPH on his 61-yard touchdown catch.

Smith-Njigba now has a catch of at least 35 yards in each of the Seahawks six games this season. It was hard to verify, but I believe that is the first time a player has done that to start a season. The last player to have at least six receptions of 35+ yards in the first six games of a season was Tyreek Hill, who had seven in 2023, but not one in every game.

Darnold and JSN and Kubiak deserve a ton of the credit for what is now the #1 ranked passing offense in the NFL by DVOA, EPA/dropback, and dropback success rate. None of it would be possible without the work of John Benton and the offensive line.

Seattle has surged into the Top 10 in opponent pressure rate and allowed pressure on just 17.2% of their dropbacks in this game. Seahawks fans have dreamed of just an average pass protecting offensive line. They now have the 3rd-youngest starting line in the league, and they are among the best at protecting the passer so far.

Run blocking remains a work in progress, but this team can win a lot of games with an elite passing offense and an elite pass rush on defense. What gets exciting is imagining what this team can look like once they get back Witherspoon and Love in the secondary and start to improve their run game.

Emmanwori is looking like a difference maker. His tackling has been excellent and his ability to rush or cover has been eye-opening. There is a whole bag of tricks Macdonald has not unveiled yet with Witherspoon still out. The interplay between Witherspoon and Emmanwori as blitz/cover/run defender options has the potential to drive offenses crazy.

It's early still, but this 2025 draft class is looking very promising, and when you throw in the free agent additions of Darnold, Lawrence, and Cooper Kupp, along with the trades of Geno Smith and DK Metcalf, this is looking like one of the best offseasons in franchise history.

Kupp continues to be an underrated signing. He had another explosive catch, himself, and also added his first touchdown of the season. He is one of the best run blockers on the team and has been mind-melding with Macdonald and Kubiak and Darnold since he arrived. It is impossible to prove just how much value he has brought to all aspects of this team, but it likely goes beyond the value of the much-criticized contract he signed.

Lawrence has been a difference maker and tone setter on the other side of the ball. This was just the second time in his last 27 games that he had multiple sacks.

The fusion of those veterans with the players like Murphy and JSN and Zabel emerging as cornerstones has changed the current and future outlook for this team.

There is no team clearly better than the Seahawks. Their offense, defense, and special teams have taken turns being the best in the NFL. Their only losses have been close games where they held the lead late against teams with a combined 9-3 record. Their three road wins have all come against teams with a winning record when they played.

If this team develops a healthy run game and returns to health in their secondary, there is every reason to put them in the conversation for the Super Bowl. They are not there yet, but they are not far from it.

The division is starting to look like a two-team race as the 49ers not only lost the game but another All-Pro defender when Fred Warner dislocated his ankle and is likely done for the season. The Rams won in Baltimore, but Puka Nacua was lost to a less serious ankle injury that may keep him out of their next game against the Jaguars in London.

Seattle gets a little extra rest as they wait to play on Monday Night Football against the Texans before their bye week. They will then travel to play the Commanders on Sunday Night Football and host the Cardinals before they finally face the Rams. Those two games against Stafford and McVay and Verse and company will likely decide the division.

Winning this game against Jacksonville was a stepping stone. There are bigger obstacles ahead that will require larger leaps. Few teams appear more ready to make those jumps than these Seahawks. ■

SEAHAWKS
88

Sam Darnold carved up the Jacksonville defense for 295 yards and two touchdowns in the 20-12 win.

SEAHAWKS 27, TEXANS 19
October 20, 2025 • Seattle, Washington

LESSONS LEARNED

DEFENSE BAILS OUT COACHES, SAM DARNOLD IN WIN OVER TEXANS

On a night when a historic managerial mistake led directly to the most painful loss in Mariners history, Mike Macdonald and Klint Kubiak said, "hold my beer."

The Seahawks built 14-0 and 27-12 leads that should have been much larger, and still tried every possible way to give the game to a vastly inferior Texans team. Seattle had four turnovers, gave up a defensive touchdown, gave away a defensive touchdown, threw interceptions by a quarterback and a receiver, had 12 penalties, and still won. That was the first time in NFL history that happened. Seattle got another dominating performance by their defense, especially the defensive line, and that was enough against a hapless Texans offense. The Seahawks are now tied for the best record in the NFC.

Seahawks fans should have known it was going to be a weird night after the first Texans possession ended in bizarre fashion. Houston quarterback, C.J. Stroud, took a snap on 3rd and 13 from his own 19-yard-line, and basically sprinted toward his own end zone to avoid a sack without realizing Uchenna Nwosu was tracking him down and tackled him in the end zone for an apparent safety. His knee went down in the end zone and the ball was in the end zone. An official initially ruled it a safety, and then some galaxy-brained referee ruled that Stroud's "forward progress" made him down at the 1-yard line. Mike Macdonald immediately threw the challenge flag, but forward progress rulings are not reviewable.

Forward progress usually involves moving forward. If a running back gets hit at the line of scrimmage and then, on his own accord, jumps backwards to try and find a hole and gets tackled five yards behind the line of scrimmage, forward progress is marked five yards back where forward progress was reestablished. Stroud never attempted to move forward and was willingly yielding ground.

That was the first of a series of bad officiating in this one. Cruelly, the same crew failed to allow the Seahawks to gain forward progress on a run later in the game when they blew the play dead despite the offensive line pushing the pile forward another 5-7 yards.

Kubiak, Sam Darnold, and the Seahawks offense were cooking early. They took the safety-that-wasn't into a quick touchdown, utilizing rookie tight end Elijah Arroyo for a big 27-yard pass and then another 8-yard throw that took them down to the 1-yard line before the offensive line scored a touchdown by pushing Zach Charbonnet over the goal line.

The defense held the Texans on 3rd and less than a yard, forcing a punt. The Seahawks offense went 80 yards on the next drive for another touchdown, keyed by a 32-yard pass to Cooper Kupp and a gorgeous touchdown throw to Jaxon Smith-Njigba. This was looking like a laugher as the

Jaxon Smith-Njigba continued his stellar play with eight catches for 123 yards and a touchdown in the win over the Texans.

11
SEAHAWKS

SEAHAWKS

Running back Ken Walker III had 17 carries for 66 yards, part of a 118 yard and two touchdown rushing attack for the Seahawks.

1st quarter ended with the Seahawks ahead 14-0 and the second quarter started with another punt from the Texans.

Tory Horton had a nifty 15-yard punt return that started a Seahawks drive at their own 43-yard line. Ken Walker III drew a 15-yard face mask and Darnold hit JSN on 19-yard pass against star cornerback Derek Stingley on 3rd and 8 to move Seattle to the Texans 21-yard-line. Then it got wacky.

Kubiak called a reverse pass with Cooper Kupp throwing to an open JSN, but the pass was way off target and was intercepted by Texans safety Calen Bullock. Certain points were pulled off the board. Houston finally got some movement on offense and kicked a field goal. Seattle came back and the wackiness continued as Jason Myers field goal was blocked. That led to another Texans field goal.

For those scoring at home, that was at least eight points taken off the board by a lost safety, a wide receiver interception, and a blocked field goal. That is often enough to cost a team a football game.

Seattle went into halftime up only eight points, and the Texans were due to get the second half kick. It was mind boggling.

Thankfully, the Texans offense was feckless, and Stroud threw a pass to Ernest Jones, who caught it while on his back. It was if Jones was telling everyone the Seahawks defense could stop the Texans in their sleep.

The resulting field goal to put Seattle up 17-6 felt insurmountable. It got even more so after Seattle stopped the Texans on 4th down the next drive, followed by another Charbonnet touchdown to go up 27-12. The Seahawks forced another three-and-out with a Ty Okada sack to end the third quarter.

All that was left to do was run out the clock. RUN out the clock.

Macdonald made a highly questionable decision to punt the ball on 4th and 1 from the Texans 44-yard line. Seattle has converted every one of the A.J. Barner tush push plays this season. They had converted one in this game. You had just rattled off a 13-yard run by Walker. Close.

Instead, Macdonald chose to do some odd punt fake in the hopes of drawing Houston offsides and then punted. The Texans returned the ball to the 21-yard line. Seattle gained 23 yards in field position. Yes, the defense had been playing lights out, but that should be an easy call to go for the first down and drain more clock. They were maybe 5-10 yards from field goal range.

It seemed to work out when the Texans could not pick up a first down. The process was still off. That will bite this team in bigger games against better opponents.

Seattle's next possession started at their own 36-yard line with roughly 12 minutes to go in the game. Easy choice to run the football. Nope. Incompletion on first down. Next play is a 16-yard run to Walker. Easy decision to run on the next play, right? Nope. Deep pass to Tory Horton was incomplete and there was a holding penalty.

Those two passes took a combined 11 seconds off the clock. The single run play took 44 seconds off the clock. There would not be another run on the series. A short pass to Charbonnet for six yards and then the fateful pass to Arroyo over the middle when he fumbled.

The Seahawks defense does their job again to stop Houston on downs. Seattle gets the ball back with less than nine minutes left in the game at their own 45-yard line. Walker breaks through for 17 yards, but they call Grey Zabel for a questionable holding penalty.

On 1st and 17, Kubiak dials up another pass over the middle instead of a high percentage screen or run play. It is intercepted. Understand that the Seahawks would have had a more positive result on these series if they simply knelt three times and punted. That has to be the mindset. Bleed the clock.

Remarkably, the defense stopped the Texans again on downs. This time, right on the goal line.

Kubiak correctly calls a run that gains a totally accepted three yards. Then, he goes back to the pass, and another deep pass at that. Incomplete. Six seconds. On 3rd and 7, deep in his own territory, knowing his quarterback already had been sacked for a touchdown, he called another pass play. Somewhere, Mike Holmgren was screaming at his television to run a draw play to Mack Strong.

Darnold made another bad decision and was sacked for what was very close to a safety. These are catastrophic mistakes. This was the Rams home loss last year all over again, except the opponent did not have Matt Stafford on the other sideline.

The Texans managed to finally score a prayer touchdown to pull within a score. A game that should have been over a half hour earlier, was somehow in question with a little over two minutes to go.

Fittingly, Kubiak finally called only run plays, and thanks to a penalty against the Texans, were able to run out the clock for a much-needed win before the bye week.

Many folks will read this and question the amount of criticism for a game where the Seahawks won handily and were clearly the better team. Houston analysts and fans are skewering their sideline for being out-schemed and out-coached. This is one of those situations where seemingly conflicting statements can all be true.

The Seahawks out schemed the Texans on both sides of the ball. The Seahawks outcoached a team that was coming off a bye week and had plenty of time to prepare. The Seahawks defense was outstanding, with special performances from a variety of players. Sam Darnold made some spectacular throws. Darnold also made the worst decisions of the season. Macdonald and Kubiak made a ton of unforced errors. The number of mistakes the Seahawks made in this game would have resulted in a loss to a lot of other football teams. The fact that they won is further evidence that their ceiling is much higher than anyone expected.

A few players that deserve a shout who have not had as much attention thus far. Nick Emmanwori is looking like the second 1st-round pick Seattle hoped he would be when they traded up to draft him in the 2nd round. Everything about him at the NFL Combine pointed to greatness. Not just his record-setting numbers, but how he carried himself and the easy confidence he displayed. Many draft analysts scoffed at him as being just a "good tester," but a problematic football player.

This was an All-American player. He was not some massive project who was a good athlete. Macdonald knew exactly how he wanted to use him and Emmanwori put it all on display Monday night.

The clip you will see countless times that had my jaw drop in real-time was when he matched slot receiver Jaylen Noel stride-for-stride 40+ yards downfield. Noel ran in the 4.3s at the combine. Emmanwori weighs at least 25 pounds more than Noel and is five inches taller. That is not supposed to be possible.

He also blitzed and pressures Stroud multiple times, made a beautiful read on a zone coverage play to break up a pass, and was stout in run defense. The NFL is learning just how big of a mistake it was to give Macdonald a nuclear weapon like Emmanwori. He can impact every facet of the defense, and this secondary has only had Love, Emmanwori, Witherspoon, and Woolen all available for four snaps the entire season. That will change after the bye week.

Drake Thomas and Okada deserve some love as well. Both impacted the game in multiple ways with tackles for loss, pass breakups and pass rush. Thomas is gaining steam as the new starter at linebacker. Okada has shown he can contribute to winning football after he has some very rough games earlier in the season.

Seattle will have a road-heavy November ahead of them, with trips to Washington, Tennessee, and Los Angeles, with a single home game against the Cardinals. The game against the Rams could very well decide the division. Macdonald and crew get the week to self-scout and make some adjustments. They will get back Robbie Ouzts, Derick Hall, Love, and Witherspoon. They may also make a trade before their next game.

This is a team that should aspire to win a ring this year. They are making youthful mistakes, both players and coaches. This defense, though, has come to play just about every single week and will keep them in games. The offense has been shockingly potent, even against the best scoring defense in the NFL. Seattle looks like a team that has less to prove about their ceiling, and more to prove about reducing self-inflicted wounds that needlessly lower their floor.

One Seattle's team came to a painful end, at least in part, due to not learning from mistakes during the season. As that season ends, a new hope rises, but only if Macdonald, Kubiak, and Darnold learn the hard lessons now. ■

FROM ADVERSITY TO GROWTH

COACH MIKE MACDONALD CONTINUES TO SHAPE TEAM IDENTITY TO PROMISING RESULTS

OCTOBER 31, 2025

Not all false starts come with a five-yard penalty. Some can cost you your job.

First-time head coaches who fail to hire the right staff in year one or build the culture and identity that reflects their vision run the risk of not seeing a year two. Mike Macdonald won 10 games in his first year in Seattle, but the product on the field did not reflect the style of play he wanted. His defense struggled to stop the run. His offense eschewed the run game altogether. The youngest head coach in the NFL (at the time) could have tried to run it back. Instead, he fired his offensive coordinator, Ryan Grubb, after just one season while making wholesale changes in personnel. The early results are promising. Macdonald has not only led the team to a 5-2 start but has done so with an emerging identity that could take them much further.

MISSION AND VISION

Walk into any boardroom in Corporate America or any early team meeting of a sports team, and you are going to hear someone talking about the importance of mission, vision, and alignment.

"That's what every team talks about in training camp," said Seahawks wide receiver, Cooper Kupp. "How are we going to establish what we're about? What's our identity? I think it's really hard because you're not playing the games. You need to play the games. You have this idea of what you're going to be, but there also has to be a willingness to adapt and move within that."

Macdonald was persistent about the vision he had for the team, even if the first season was a detour in some respects. He used the offseason to create a more shared understanding of where they were versus where they needed to go. A key moment happened in Mobile, Alabama.

One benefit of an unhappy early end to the 2024 season was the space it created for Macdonald to travel with President of Football Operations & General Manager, John Schneider, to the Senior Bowl. He was able to meet with prospects and watch them practice, but most importantly, he was able to spend that time with the personnel department.

Macdonald surprised the scouts by walking them through a position-by-position review of the current roster. He shared where he saw strength, and where he saw a need to improve. He opened by expressing enthusiasm for the opportunity in front of them.

"I love this shit," Macdonald said. "This is an opportunity to become the team we want to be."

The scouting department appreciated the honesty and humility he demonstrated by not only calling out personnel improvements that were needed, but better coaching as well. In this small town, at a small school, thousands of miles from team headquarters, Macdonald took the first step toward building a much different second season.

"That was awesome," said director of college scouting Aaron Hineline. "It was real. Anytime you have that level of communication and honesty, you know where you stand. And our players are getting that too. I thought that was great. It was unfiltered, it was refreshing, because there's not too many times that that happens."

It was on that same field that Macdonald and Schneider watched the player who would become their first pick in the

Head coach Mike Macdonald took the lessons he learned in his first season with Seattle in 2024 to help take the franchise to the next level.

draft, Grey Zabel, dominate every pass rusher who challenged him, from nearly every position on the offensive line.

One small trip to Mobile, Alabama. One large leap for Seahawk-kind. Macdonald did not rest there.

During an era when coaches like Sean McVay and Kyle Shanahan skip the NFL Scouting Combine, Macdonald and members of his coaching staff attended for the week. He sat in on all the visits with prospects. He watched players go through drills. His new quarterbacks coach, Andrew Janocko, worked out the QBs on the field. It was there that Macdonald first met the player who he pushed hard to take with what became their second selection, Nick Emmanwori.

The 21-year-old man-child stood 6'3" and weighed 220 pounds. He had grown up playing cornerback before "outgrowing" the position and being moved to safety. He put on a show during the workouts, touching the sky with a 43" vertical, bounding over 11 feet in the broad jump, and then impossibly registering a 4.38 40-yard-dash to cement what would become the new relative athletic standard for the safety position, ranking 1st of 1,086 players who had tested since 1987.

Many draft analysts questioned whether Emmanwori could play safety in the NFL. There were some who had a 3rd round grade on him despite his overwhelming athleticism and All-American recognition for play on the field. Macdonald had a vision for how he could unlock things for his defense. Schneider and Macdonald considered taking him with their first-round pick but were thrilled to wind up with two players they considered first-round talents on either side of the ball.

CRISIS BECOMES OPPORTUNITY

Free agency was a little more complicated. Macdonald and Schneider had every intention to bring back Geno Smith and D.K. Metcalf. Both were due new deals. Both were tone setters in the locker room and on the field, though that tone was not always aligned with where Macdonald was leading. Both decided they would rather play elsewhere.

What could have been a crisis, may have been good fortune. Instead of bringing back two prominent players who clearly were not bought in to the new direction Macdonald represented, the slate was wiped clean. Each were traded for draft picks.

The knock-on effects were significant. All the money that had been earmarked to their sizable contract requirements was now available to be spent elsewhere. Some was spent on new quarterback, Sam Darnold. Darnold was almost a decade younger than Smith, less expensive, and was excited to be a part of the team. Cooper Kupp, a native of Washington and renowned standard setter with his work ethic, stepped into the wide receiver room. DeMarcus Lawrence was contemplating retirement, but was convinced to rejoin defensive coordinator Aden Durde, who he knew from their days together in Dallas. Lawrence had slowed as a pass rusher but was still a dominating run defender and like Kupp, was known to be a tremendous worker and leader.

The pick acquired in the Metcalf trade was used as part of a package to move up for Emmanwori. The pick acquired for Smith was used on QB Jalen Milroe, who was taken to develop behind Darnold. The extra picks may have also played a role in Schneider feeling comfortable taking Zabel in the first round, knowing he had the ammunition to move around the draft board on the second day of the draft.

Seattle had become younger and cheaper at quarterback, while marrying a historically athletic rookie class with some thoughtful veteran additions. The players getting paid the most all wanted to be here and were exemplary workers and leaders. Now it was up to Macdonald to mold this group into one capable of kicking down the door to the playoffs and winning their first playoff game since 2019.

FORGING THE NEW CULTURE

On the advice of Schneider, the Seahawks coach reached out to performance psychologist, Dr. Michael Gervais, who was a key figure in the early days of the Pete Carroll era in Seattle. He worked with coaches and players to help maximize their careers. Macdonald wanted help reaching the team and opened himself up to having his team meetings recorded and reviewed by Gervais and his team for feedback.

"As a head coach, where do I fall short," Macdonald said on a podcast with former Seahawk Richard Sherman. "Well, I can be better in these areas, you know, like streamlining the message, taking more ownership of the team, being better in the team meetings, connecting the building better, having better relationships with our players. All those things were a priority."

Asking your players to grow and be their best hits differently when the head coach is asking the same of himself. Macdonald knew the message had to be amplified by more than just his voice. Players needed to be the standard bearers. They had to understand and care about the vision enough to hold each other accountable. This was not about individual position groups. The goal was to create a locker room where everyone felt comfortable approaching each other. Macdonald set out to build mechanisms to help foster that connection.

Players were asked to share their "why" in front of their teammates, explaining why they pursue this violent and short-lived career beyond the money.

"I think something that's been cool and part of growing the connection has been having guys go up and explain why they love football and why they show up every day," Leonard Williams said during minicamp in June. "They put up pictures of their family and pictures of them when they were young."

Williams went on to explain how that helped beyond team meetings.

"Obviously, going through camp is going to be hard. Everyone has tough days," Williams said. "And now if I see someone having a hard or tough day, I understand that guy a little deeper now, on a human level, and I know his 'why' now, and how to talk to him and push him a little better."

Williams was one of the only players to share his why outside of the meetings.

"Football has given me everything," Williams explained. "I grew up homeless at times, in and out of hotels, motels, and an unstable lifestyle as a young kid. When I found football, it gave me stability and good male role models, and kind of distracted me from everything going on at home. I fell in love with the camaraderie and the team aspect."

Team outings to Top Golf and to the premiere of Mission: Impossible were interspersed with intense and physical practices to provide more opportunities for casual and genuine relationships to grow. Players broke out into groups that crossed position room boundaries and sides of the ball, allowing unlikely bonds to form. Guys would take "Walk and Talks" along Lake Washington just to get to know each other.

"We would just get to know people," Jarran Reed said. "Believe it or not, Michael [Dickson], our punter, we were on a walk and talk and I knew he was competitive, but I didn't realize he takes it to heart like he does. How much pride he takes in doing his job made me look at him in a different sort of way."

Where many NFL locker rooms are organized by position group and side of the ball (e.g., tight ends together and near the offense), Seattle mixed up assignments so these uncommon bonds could continue to build. Edge rusher Uchenna Nwosu dresses next to offensive lineman Charles Cross. Fullback Robbie Ouzts is neighbors with receiver Tory Horton. Tight end Elijah Arroyo is close to quarterbacks Darnold and Milroe.

"This is probably the most time in a locker room I have seen offensive line interacting with defensive backs, defensive line interacting with receivers, quarterbacks," Reed said. "Everyone talks to everyone on this team. It's been a minute since I've seen that in a locker room. Everyone is building a bond with each other."

That showed up in practices as well when Williams would pull rookie Zabel aside during one-versus-one pass rush drills and give him tips about how to improve his pass protection. The pair have continued those conversations into the season.

No matter how clear the messaging is or how much a leader works to create a positive environment, it ultimately is up to the players to decide whether they care enough about team goals to make some personal sacrifices. One crucial demonstration of that personal sacrifice is participation in optional OTA sessions during the spring.

It is common for some players to skip these workouts or practices in order to spend more time with their friends and family, or just enjoy the offseason. Metcalf, for example, missed large portions of the OTAs in 2024.

Not this group. The Seahawks had close to 100% participation throughout the spring. It allowed for those relationships to deepen between players, between coaches, and throughout the organization.

Veterans like Kupp and rookies like Emmanwori used some of the time to pick Macdonald's brain in his office, and vice versa. Macdonald would run defensive concepts by Kupp to see what an offensive mind thought. Kupp's knowledge of division rival Sean McVay was not going to go unused. Emmanwori had such a voracious appetite for time with Macdonald that the coach started wondering if he should close the door now and then. Kupp noted how that open-door approach has deepened the connection with the players.

"I have rarely been up in the coaches' offices and seen his door closed," Kupp said. "If guys want to go up and ask questions or if they want to be around their coaches and figure things out, his door is open. He wants to be around guys. He's out there in the hallways and his access isn't turned off. I think that goes a long way in terms of being able to connect with guys when there is so much on his plate as the head coach. Even the defensive stuff, but also as a head coach in general where he has to handle all the logistical stuff as well. He's never going to turn down a conversation."

The connections were developing. The message was getting through. The scouting department had added custom-fit parts through the draft and free agency to meet glaring needs. Everything appeared to be coming together. As the great philosopher Mike Tyson once said, though, "everyone has a plan until they get punched in the mouth."

The next test would be whether all the words and all the practice reps against teammates would translate into performance on the field during the regular season. It did not start well.

WEEK ONE: FAILURE TO LAUNCH

The San Francisco 49ers have dominated the Seahawks for the past few seasons. Seattle finally broke through for a win in Santa Clara last year, but both clubs were looking to make a statement to start 2025.

Macdonald had been deliberate in his search for a new offensive coordinator. He did not want to risk winding up in the same situation where he and his most important coaching partner were not on the same page. Klint Kubiak came from a long line of coaches who built their offense around the run game and play-action counters.

Kubiak made it clear from his first press conference that this would be a team that utilized outside zone runs to set up everything else. There were reasons heading into the first game to believe the running game would get off to a strong start.

His young offensive line had looked fantastic in clearing holes during the preseason, even topping 200 rushing yards in one game. The 49ers had won just six games the previous season and had lost a lot of talent on the defensive side of the ball. Their replacements were young and unproven.

Luckily for San Francisco, Robert Saleh had fallen into their laps as a defensive coordinator after a failed stint in New York and an about-face from Liam Coen, who took the Jacksonville job before they moved on to Saleh.

What looked to be the first test of the new Seahawks offensive identity never materialized. Kubiak did attempt to run the ball, but it was ineffective. All the work the team had done from under center and on play-action was largely ignored in the game plan. The offense operated primarily out of the shotgun and attempted only one play-action pass, dead last in the NFL in that first week. Most of the passes that were thrown were quick screens to the perimeter that went nowhere, and often lost yards. For Seattle fans, it felt like a nightmarish combination of the worst of Shane Waldron and Grubb.

Saleh may have taken them out of some of what they wanted to do, but a true identity for a football team is persistent across opponents. This felt more like a violation of one of Macdonald's core mantras, "through, not around."

It was puzzling to see Kubiak go away from the offensive identity so quickly and completely. One of the criticisms of Grubb was that he seemed to adjust his approach each week instead of having a core philosophy he forced others to stop.

It was not surprising to see an offense struggle with a new coaching staff, a new scheme, and fresh personnel. Seeing them betray their identity so quickly, though, was a red flag.

Despite the offense failing to find itself, the defense and special teams helped the Seahawks hold a lead until the 49ers final drive. Crucial mistakes by cornerback Tariq Woolen led to a go-ahead touchdown, followed by a strip sack of Darnold after he had led the team quickly into the red zone with a chance to win.

Seattle would fall on that day to their bitter rival in painful fashion. They would later find out injury was added to insult when top player Devon Witherspoon was lost with a bruised MCL and Emmanwori had a high ankle sprain.

It was another false start, and one that stung after all that had been done to get to this point. The question was no longer whether they had an identity, but whether they had the conviction to stick with it.

OFFENSIVE IDENTITY: HEAVY PERSONNEL, RUN, & EXPLOSIVE PLAY-ACTION

Macdonald took the loss hard. He admitted to being "edgy" all week. Part of the frustration almost certainly was losing without "throwing their fastball," a phrase Macdon-

Mike Macdonald took steps to boost Seattle's offense in his second year at the helm, including developing Jaxson Smith-Njigba from a burgeoning young Pro Bowl receiver to arguably the best at the position in the league.

SMITH-NJIGBA
11

ald often utters to indicate a desire to always play to their strengths. He was asked about the lack of play-action passes and his answer was terse, but clear.

"We need to [play] action more," Macdonald said. "We need more [pocket] movement. We'll call it. We'll execute it when called."

The game appeared to be a wakeup call for Kubiak. Lose or win, they were going to play their style. No longer would he allow an opponent to dictate terms to him or let his game plan stray too far from their core philosophy.

Over 30% of Darnold's pass attempts have been play-action in the six weeks that followed, ranking 5th-highest in the NFL. He has averaged a league-leading 15.0 yards per attempt on play-action passes and has the highest grade (93.3) of any starting quarterback on those throws by Pro Football Focus (PFF).

The most consistent beneficiary has been receiver Jaxon Smith-Njigba (JSN). Nature abhors a vacuum, and apparently, so does Smith-Njigba. He more than filled the void left by Metcalf. His efficiency has been off the charts. Every box has been checked. A player who many had pegged as a slot receiver with good hands shattered every preconceived notion. He has beaten teams inside, outside, short, intermediate, and deep. No receiver has been more explosive than Smith-Njigba through seven games. His stellar play was recognized with a NFC Offensive Player of the Month award for October.

Part of that success has come from Kubiak. He hand-picked Ouzts to be his fullback in the draft, with an eye on playing more 21 personnel (2 backs, 1 TE). He helped recruit Eric Saubert, who he had experience with in Denver, to improve the blocking of the tight end room and allow them to play more 12 personnel (1 back, 2 TEs).

These personnel packages have led the Seahawks to face more base defensive personnel from opposing defenses. Most teams have optimized their rosters to play nickel defenses the vast majority of the time. Being forced to put an extra linebacker on the field and pulling off a nickel corner often means swapping in a lesser player who has fewer reps.

Kubiak has used motion to create overloads on one side of the formation that can cause a safety to rotate down near the line of scrimmage. Seattle is facing more stacked boxes (8+ defenders near the line of scrimmage) than any other offense in the NFL (38.1%), per Next Gen Stats. That is leading to more single high safety looks, further advantaging the passing game.

It has made for tougher sledding in the run game, where Seattle ranks near the bottom of the league in efficiency. Being the most explosive passing team in the NFL, however, has probably been more than worth the slow start on the ground. The commitment to the run that looks exactly the same as a play-action pass has made the Seahawks a top-five scoring offense.

Even if overall run game has not got untracked, there are signs that the physical identity Macdonald wants is taking hold. Seattle was a terrible short yardage team a year ago. They had trouble converting and often chose to pass instead of run. The change in year two has been drastic.

In fact, when narrowing to just rushing attempts on 3rd or 4th down with 1 yard to go, the Seahawks have a better conversion rate (87.5%) than the tush-pushing Philadelphia Eagles (86.7%). Seattle has converted every time they have utilized tight end A.J. Barner in their version of the tush push. The only time they have not converted a 3rd or 4th and 1 run play was when they ran out of shotgun with Zach Charbonnet.

The best of what Seattle has to offer might be their 12 personnel package that is first in the NFL in EPA/play, and has been efficient in both the run and pass. Kubiak has also shown no clear tendency when in that group, as the pass/run rate is roughly 50/50.

All of this has helped to raise the level of what has been a beleaguered offensive line. Darnold is also getting rid of the ball faster than he ever has in his career. A healthy Abe Lucas at right tackle has been key, after spending most of the past two seasons with second and third-string players at that position. One of the most important changes has been how the scheme is keeping defenses guessing on when they can safely rush the passer.

Committing to the run forces defenders to account for that before the snap. The dangerous play-action game puts some hesitation in the minds of defensive linemen. Movement of the pocket with bootlegs and rollouts changes where the target will be. All of these strategies keep pass rushers from being able to consistently anticipate a pass and pin their ears back to rush the quarterback.

The result? Darnold has been sacked just 9 times in his first seven games after being sacked 9 times in his final game with the Vikings.

Kubiak's offense has become consistent, productive, and explosive. Young players are making leaps, and there is room for more growth from rookies like tight end Elijah

Arroyo and Horton. If Seattle can find a more productive rushing attack on early downs, they will be as dangerous as any offense in the league.

Underlying the success has been a clarity about who they want to be and how they want to play. Even if not all parts of the vision are realized, it is easy to see the outline of what they want to be. Kubiak and his staff are in their first season here, and he has never had a chance to be in the same place for more than one season as the offensive coordinator due to his head coaches being let go. While some may assume he would jump at a head coaching opportunity if one came his way, there is reason to believe he might choose some stability for him and his family.

In some ways, he is ahead of his boss. Macdonald took eight games to get his defense and personnel in place with Baltimore and again with Seattle. Kubiak had one game to forget. Macdonald had many more last season. That adversity has led to growth.

"You probably learn way more from stubbing your toe than you do with having success," Kubiak said when asked about the 49ers game.

Macdonald had a much stronger hand to start this season given his head start last year, but the injuries against San Francisco created an early obstacle he would have to overcome.

DEFENSIVE IDENTITY: TRENCHES & BOXES

Schneider hired Macdonald, in part, due to the identity he established on the defensive side in Baltimore. Seattle currently sits 5-2. The last time they were 5-2 was in 2023 when they traded for Williams ahead of a game with the Ravens in Baltimore. Macdonald's defense confused and overwhelmed the Seahawks on that day in a 37-3 drubbing. Schneider took note and would hire Macdonald just a couple of months later.

A consistent thread across Macdonald's defenses has been an ability to create pressure with just four players. He rarely blitzes, which allows the team to keep more players available in coverage. The creativity of who is coming on those pressure packages has led to one of the highest rates of unblocked rushers over his career.

Getting to those pressures, though, requires a sturdy run defense. Seattle struggled mightily in that regard last season. After a decent start, there was a five-week stretch where they were the worst run defense in football. They allowed at least 155 yards on the ground in four of the five games, including 175 yards against the lowly Giants in Lumen Field, which resulted in the most embarrassing loss of the season.

Macdonald prefers to play light boxes (6 or fewer defenders near the line of scrimmage). This allows more players to remain in coverage and creates fewer openings for the passing game. The problem was that Seattle could not stop the run in those looks.

That led to ejecting the two starting inside linebackers off the team during the season last year. Schneider was able to orchestrate a trade for Ernest Jones IV, who became an instant leader and stabilizing force. Still, the run defense buckled in a game against the Green Bay Packers that ended a four-game winning streak.

Seattle would finish 22nd in the NFL in yards per carry allowed (4.9 YPC) when in light boxes, and 15th in EPA/rush in those situations. They rank 2nd (3.4 YPC) and 1st in those categories, respectively, this season. There has not been a better run defense in the NFL in 2025.

The addition of Lawrence has been critical. He not only is one of the best edge setters in the league, but he can move inside and is strong enough to hold up there against interior linemen. A return to health for Uchenna Nwosu has been a big lift as well.

Nwosu was always an exceptional run defender and has also made an instant impact as a pass rusher with 5.0 sacks in the past four games.

Byron Murphy II was solid as a rookie, but rarely got a chance to stay on the field for pass rushing situations. He has continued to be a force against the run and is the rare player able to generate pass pressure from the nose tackle position.

Williams continues to play at an All-Pro level, with Reed next to him as one of the more underrated defenders in the league. Derick Hall and Boye Mafe have contributed as both run defenders and pass rushers as well.

The rotation at defensive tackle and edge is as strong as the Seahawks have seen in some time.

That dominant front has allowed Seattle to weather a storm from the injuries that hit the secondary early in the year. Witherspoon and Emmanwori were lost in week one, while safety Julian Love was lost in week two.

There was one game, against Baker Mayfield and the Bucs, where the defense buckled. They played without Lawrence, Witherspoon, and Love. Hall and Tariq Woolen went down with injuries during the game. The Bucs are the only team to score more than 20 points against Seattle, and only the second team to gain more than 300 yards.

The injuries have tested Macdonald's mettle. Witherspoon, Love, and Emmanwori were central to his plan to defend the run without sacrificing coverage. He never flinched, even after the blowup against Tampa. With roughly the same secondary players available to him the following week in a game against the 4-1 Jacksonville Jaguars who had just taken down the 49ers and Kansas City Chiefs in back-to-back weeks, his defense dominated.

An early miscommunication in the secondary led to a touchdown that looked a lot like the Bucs game, but those would be the only points the Jaguars would get until the fourth quarter.

The one constant this season has been the run defense. Seattle has gone six straight games allowing fewer than 90 yards rushing, and the last three games without allowing more than 60 yards on the ground. Their weakness from last season has become a strength.

And now some of the key injured players are returning. Emmanwori has played so well in his three games that his odds of winning Defensive Rookie of the Year have skyrocketed. Lawrence has had 3.0 sacks in his two games since he returned to the field. Woolen has steadied after a rough start. Witherspoon is expected to play against the Commanders for the first time in four weeks, and only his third game this season.

They have been the 3rd-best defense in the NFL by DVOA, and also rank 3rd in yards per play allowed. There is every reason to believe they can be even better when they get their starters back. Williams was prophetic during training camp about how they would need to overcome adversity, and pointed back to bonds built over the offseason as the key to pulling through.

"We definitely let some games slip out of our hands last year," Williams said. "I think having a clearer identity as a team will help us push through those hard times that we went through last season. Me and Julian (Love) talked about this actually, where, every great team, every team in general, is going to go through at least two hard points in the season, and it's the great ones who can bounce back, and rely on their culture, rely on their training, that would be able to push through those hard moments and make it through the playoffs and further."

IT'S ALL ABOUT THE FINISH

Macdonald came to Seattle with a reputation as a schematic whiz kid. He proved that it was transferable even when taking on head coaching duties. The Seahawks finished last season with one of the best defenses in football and a middling offense that was orthogonal to Macdonald's vision. He was not satisfied with winning 10 games or narrowly missing out on the division title.

The investments he made from January to June—closing gaps with scouting, aligning his staff, and forging a new culture with his players—have paid off. Great teams know who they are. They are the lion who hides from no one and makes others wary, not the chameleon who tries to blend in.

Macdonald's first season was a 10-win false start. The Week 1 loss to San Francisco was another. Both were costly, but neither proved fatal. The identity he and Schneider forged in Mobile, cemented in Indianapolis, and nurtured on walks along Lake Washington is no longer just a vision. It's a 5-2 reality, built on a dominant defense and an explosive, physical offense.

Whether that identity is capable of winning a Super Bowl will be decided in January and February. But after a year of resetting the standard, the Seahawks are no longer waiting for the play to start.

The whistle has blown. This time, there are no flags on the field. ■

There were a lot of smiles from Mike Macdonald on the way to a 14-3 regular season and the number one seed in the NFC.

FOX SPORTS
FOX SPORTS
SEATTLE SEAHAWKS

SEAHAWKS 38, COMMANDERS 14
November 2, 2025 • Landover, Maryland

FROM GOOD TO GREAT

SUBLIME SAM DARNOLD LEADS DRUBBING OF COMMANDERS

Vincent van Gogh only sold one painting while alive. Emily Dickinson had fewer than a dozen of her thousands of poems published during her lifetime. Greatness is often easier to recognize given the benefit of context and reflection. The more unexpected the source of the splendor, the longer it takes to be embraced.

The 2025 Seattle Seahawks are a work of art. What makes them special is not simply the sublime blending of young and old, power and precision, simple and complex. It is the collection of second-hand parts, who have been overlooked and underestimated. Sam Darnold is doing things the NFL has not seen since peak Tom Brady. Jaxon Smith-Njigba is doing things not seen since Calvin Johnson. Leonard Williams is wrecking lines like Tony Montana. These are just a few of the men on this team who have been cast aside, played second fiddle, or deemed lesser than they are. Collectively, they were expected to win seven or eight games. Collectively, they are The Starry Night, the perfect poem, the unforgettably forgotten. Outside praise has come through clenched teeth. That's okay. This team is happy to knock a few loose.

Seahawks fans have seen their team rise before. The 2005 squad won 11 straight games. The 2012 team exploded for wins of 58-0, 50-17, and then 42-13 over their most bitter division rival. Both were Seahawks teams, but saying they were the same would be like saying California and Alabama are the same because they are part of the same country. Each team has its own DNA. Their destiny is partly nature and partly nurture. An inescapable part of this team's story is how little people outside the organization thought of them before the season.

They were expected to win seven or eight games. The only reason Darnold's deal was considered palatable was because Seattle could "get out of it" after one season. Sean McVay and Kyle Shanahan's offenses were what the league should fear, not Mike Macdonald's defense. Smith-Njigba was only a slot receiver and not true number one receiver material. The offensive line was destined to be near the bottom of the NFL again. Klint Kubiak was a mediocre nepotism hire. Uchenna Nwosu was too injured, too often. Byron Murphy II was a not worth a first round pick. Josh Jobe was a weak spot in the secondary. A.J. Barner and the tight end room was not talented enough.

To say they were overlooked would be inaccurate. They were considered and roundly dismissed as not worthy. There has never been a Seahawks team that has so completely outpaced expectations as this crew has done so far.

Consider that their +81-point differential is the highest in the history of the franchise through eight games, besting the 2013 Seahawks by one point. The 2005 squad is third (+68). They are close to their projected win total (7.5 games) with half the season left to play. They have not

Seahawks wide receiver Tory Horton makes a touchdown catch against the Washington Commanders. Quarterback Sam Darnold connected with his receivers for four touchdowns in the first half alone.

Running back Zach Charbonnet leaps to evade the Washington Commanders' defense during a first-half carry.

KINLAW
99

lost on the road this season and have won 10 straight away from Seattle. They are the top ranked DVOA team, and the only team that ranks in the top five in offense, defense, and special teams. They are 5th in points scored and 5th in points allowed. They are 2nd in yard per play, and 3rd in opponent yards per play. That questionable offensive line has paved the way to the 5th-best opponent pressure rate while the defensive line has powered them to the 2nd-best pressure rate on the other side of the ball.

This team has lost players like Devon Witherspoon, Julian Love, DeMarcus Lawrence, Tariq Woolen, Robbie Ouzts, Derick Hall, and Cooper Kupp without losing their mojo.

Macdonald is cooking people on defense while Kubiak dishes the second course of butt whooping on offense. Jay Harbaugh finishes the meal with a dessert of mascot brûlée.

The signs have been there all season. Seattle has only two losses, to two winning teams, by a combined total of seven points. They should have beaten the Steelers, Jaguars, and Texans by many more points than they did. As good of a meal as the Seahawks coaches have been cooking, the team has played with their food far too often.

It would have been understandable if this was the latest game for the Seahawks to allow an inferior team to make fans sweat. The Commanders were playing for their season in front of their home crowd on primetime. They had their dynamic quarterback in the lineup, and most of their key players were able to return from injury to start the game. Dan Quinn is a great motivator, and Seattle was making a long trip after a bye week.

Bettors seemed to be wary as the game drew near, as the line moved from Seattle -3.5 to -2.5 before kickoff. The folks who caused those lines to move lost a lot of money Sunday night.

The Seahawks put together one of the most dominant games in franchise history. It started with a first drive that actually covered more than 100 yards. Officially, it was a 90-yard touchdown drive that took over eight minutes, but multiple penalties meant it took Seattle 104 yards of offense to complete the task. The team overcame a 1st and 25 and a 2nd and 17 with relative ease. It was a sign of things to come.

Washington had no answers for what Kubiak and Darnold threw their way. The Seahawks offense has excelled this season in 12 and 21 personnel groupings where extra tight ends or a fullback are on the field to force defenses to match with heavier, slower, players, and taking more defenders out of coverage to defend the run. It stood to reason that the team would lean into that even more with starting receiver Kupp out for the first time this year. Kubiak did the exact opposite.

Seattle utilized three receivers more often, especially in the first half. In fact, it was their highest percentage of 11 personnel usage in the first half this season.

First Half 11 Personnel Usage by Week:
- **Week 1:** 44.4% (12 of 27 plays)
- **Week 2:** 36.4% (12 of 33 plays)
- **Week 3:** 30.0% (6 of 20 plays)
- **Week 4:** 13.3% (4 of 30 plays)
- **Week 5:** 54.2% (13 of 24 plays)
- **Week 6:** 50.0% (12 of 24 plays)
- **Week 7:** 45.2% (14 of 31 plays)
- **Week 9:** 55.6% (15 of 27 plays)

His receivers and his quarterback rewarded him with a firework show fitting for the nation's capital. Tory Horton Jr. caught the first two touchdown passes. Cody White caught his first career touchdown on a 60-yard strike that had Commanders fans mumbling to themselves in their seats. In between, tight end Elijah Arroyo caught his first career touchdown.

Darnold authored a first half that was as good as any in NFL history. He was 16-16 for 284 yards, an incomprehensible 17.6 yards per attempt, four touchdowns, zero interceptions and a perfect passer rating. The last time a quarterback had four touchdowns on his first four drives without an incomplete pass was Tom Brady in 2007. Fitting, considering Brady was the person who convinced the Raiders not to sign Darnold this offseason.

Blowouts are not just the product of explosive offense. Separation comes from all phases contributing. The defense dominated a motivated Commanders offense. Jayden Daniels was pressured on over 50% of his dropbacks, the highest rate of his career. Ty Okada had a gorgeous interception. Coverage was smothering, even after Jobe was lost due to a friendly fire hit that led to some concussion concerns. Nick Emmanwori was the latest Seahawk to manhandle two opponents on one play. Ouzts and Barner have blocked multiple guys to key big plays. Williams has tossed multiple offensive linemen ten yards back to free up others for sacks. Emmanwori drove a blocker into the backfield and then wrapped one arm around the ball carrier with the other arm around the blocker for the best kind of bear hug. It was a play that would have made Kam Chancellor proud.

Meanwhile, Brandon Pili, was charging down the field on kick coverage at the behest of Harbaugh. The rare sight of a 330+ pound nose tackle on special teams looked like a stroke of brilliance when Pili forced a fumble on a kickoff that was recovered by the Seahawks and quickly turned into the Arroyo touchdown.

Macdonald asked the team after the win over the Texans to imagine what it would be like when all three phases are working in the same game. They did not have to wait long to turn that dream into reality.

Two straight primetime games. Two straight convincing performances. Three thousand miles and two weeks apart. Some key players exit. Others return. The style of play remains the same.

Younger Seattle Mariners fans hate when older fans always reference the 1995 season. The idea that the team's best years are long past, and their most iconic stars are irreplaceable can be aggravating and depressing. The same applies to the Seahawks Super Bowl teams of 2005, 2013, and 2014. The Legion of Boom, especially, was one of the best teams of the modern NFL era.

Just like the 2025 Mariners started to write their own storyline with their own iconic stars, this Seahawks team is making it harder for fans to yearn for the good ol' days. The present is proving to be worth every bit of your attention.

One thing that ties all great teams together is that they must pass a crucible of increasingly difficult tests to earn a spot in history. This Seahawks team has passed a number of tests. Many remain. None bigger than the game in two weeks against the Rams in Los Angeles. These division rivals do not only look like the two best teams in their division, they may be the two best teams in football.

Macdonald was sometimes called the "McVay of defense." The rest of this season could have teams looking for the next Macdonald.

Part of climb from obscurity to championship contender includes passing through the inflection point where national voices go from doubting to lauding. Little or no expectation turn into high expectations with more scrutiny. There will be more interview requests, more schematic dissections, more friends, and family coming out of the woodwork.

This team is better equipped than most to handle that transition due to the work Macdonald and team did this offseason to foster clarity, identity, and connection. It does not make them impervious to what is ahead. The change is a little like equalizing pressure for divers coming up from depth. The faster the ascent, the bigger the chance you get the bends. Seattle's rise is going to go subsonic after this win.

Now we see what John Schneider and Macdonald do with this fast start. There are indications they will be active before the trade deadline on Tuesday. There is not the same desperate need to address on this roster as there have been on some others that have led Schneider to make a move. We will learn more about the injury to Ernest Jones in the days ahead, but that is one to watch. Macdonald, for what it's worth, did not seem overly concerned about the Jones knee injury after the game.

The Seahawks could go after help on the interior offensive line, linebacker, edge rush, cornerback, wide receiver, or even safety. None of those areas are in terrible shape. Each might benefit from more depth.

An artist is sometimes best served from putting the brush down. A poet can benefit from fewer words. And sometimes, it's that final brush stroke or stanza that turns a great work into a masterpiece. Hindsight won't be necessary to appreciate this Seahawks team. Open your eyes. It's a new day in Seattle. ■

SEAHAWKS 26, VIKINGS 0
November 30, 2025 • Seattle, Washington

SHUT 'EM DOWN

SEATTLE DOMINATES MINNESOTA FOR FIRST SHUTOUT IN TEN YEARS

A manager once told me the mark of a great leader is the variety of people that person can guide to success. It not nearly as difficult to do great things when all parts of an organization are performing at a high level, as it is when there are pockets of mediocrity.

Football has a similar reality. The game is easy when every part of the team is excelling. Ask the Saints or the Commanders how it feels when this Seahawks squad has everything working. There will be games where the offense, defense, or special teams are not performing to their standard. The mark of a great team is their ability to win a wide variety of games. Seattle saw their top-ranked passing game grounded against the Vikings but were able to still dominate thanks to stellar defensive performance, a great day from special teams, and a solid running game.

It is natural to be concerned about how inept the passing game was for Seattle. Pass protection was atrocious, especially in the first half, when Darnold was sacked four times and fumbled twice. There will be those who look at this performance and the disaster against the Rams as reasons for pessimism about where this team will go. The reality is that if Darnold had taken four sacks in that game in Los Angeles, they probably would have won.

Mike Macdonald appeared to have a similar perspective after the game when said Darnold, "took some good sacks actually in some of those critical moments, which is good team football." Had Darnold tried to toss the ball into harm's way instead of taking those sacks, this game could have gone differently.

There is no way the game against the Rams did not impact Darnold's confidence and that of his coaches. This three-game stretch against bad football teams that have defenses capable of pressuring the quarterback is a chance to try and work through some of what ails him.

Minnesota is a unique defensive team with a one-of-a-kind defensive coordinator. Brian Flores blitzes at the highest rate in football, and from unorthodox places and pre-snap looks. The notion that they gave the rest of the league a blueprint for how to play Darnold is as silly as when people said Chris Shula found kryptonite with his heavy use of dime personnel. Very few teams can mimic what either opponent did.

What could transfer is the exploiting of a protection flaw in the Seahawks blitz pickup. There was controversy a year ago in San Francisco that Kyle Shanahan did not give Brock Purdy flexibility to adjust protections at the line. Other teams were getting better at decoding those protections and making big plays at big moments.

Klint Kubiak comes from that lineage, as does John Benton. There may be some adjustments they need to make

Defensive end Marcus Lawrence forces a fumble by Vikings running back Aaron Jones Sr. en route to a historic shutout win.

Seahawks

HOME

Zach Charbonnet finds a clear path to the end zone during the second half, adding to the Seahawks' considerable victory margin.

to keep teams from taking advantage of their protection rules. There were some decent adjustments in the second half when there were more passes to the flat and quick screens. Darnold was not sacked after halftime.

The best way to not get sacked or throw an interception is to run the football. Seattle did a credible job on the ground, rushing for 125 yards, their fourth-straight game over 110 yards. They had two more explosive rushes, bringing their total to 15 in the last four games, ranking 5th in the NFL over that stretch. Their 572 yards rushing since Week 10 ranks 4th in the NFL.

Macdonald and Kubiak know they can cook with early play-action and deep explosive passes. They are in the lab tinkering to find other ways they can win when the game requires a different style of play. Getting a reliable run game would be ideal. Adding a quality screen game would be another useful tool.

The last time a Seahawks team shutout an opponent was also a 26-0 game at home where the offense only managed one touchdown. That was the 2015 squad, during Tyler Lockett's rookie year. Lockett took a kickoff 105 yards back for a touchdown, and Richard Sherman returned a punt 65 yards. Russell Wilson was sacked four times. The opposing quarterback was an overmatched young backup. Sound familiar?

Max Brosmer walked into Lumen Field as an undrafted rookie free agent who many in Minnesota and around the league were eager to see take the helm after the poor play of J.J. McCarthy. DeMarcus Lawrence, Ernest Jones, and company made sure he left Seattle battered and broken.

Time after time, we have seen unheralded, or just plain bad quarterbacks, play over their heads against the Seahawks. The Giants shamed Seattle twice, first with Colt McCoy in 2020, and then with Daniel Jones last season. Case Keenum did with the Rams against that 2015 squad. Austin Davis beat the LOB in 2014 with the Rams. It does not seem to matter how many times that happens. Many fans still discount a dominant defensive performance against a bad quarterback. Not here.

Holding a team to zero points is a huge achievement no matter who is on the other side of the ball. Taking the ball away five times is impressive work. Scoring on defense is rare and should be celebrated without qualification.

A Seahawks linebacker outscored the entire Vikings offense, and nearly gained more yards. Jones finished with 91 yards on his two interceptions. Minnesota finished with 96 yards passing. They had 87 total yards of offense early in the 4th quarter before some garbage time yards boosted their total to 162 for the game.

Seattle's defense was as complete as it has been in a long time. Every starter on defense was available outside of Julian Love. It showed.

There was nowhere to go for the Vikings offense. They could not run outside or inside. How overmatched were they in the run game? Minnesota had 10 yards on 10 carries until late in the 4th quarter. They could not beat pressure with quick passes. The Seahawks secondary swarmed everything in front of them. And when they did ask Brosmer to push the ball past the line of scrimmage, a fiendish collage of off-target throws, painful sacks, and awful interceptions joined to create nightmares that will haunt his sleep for a long time.

Lawrence has been so much more than a tone setter and a leader on this defense. He has been one of their best and most impactful players. The play he made on Brosmer on a 4th down in the Vikings lone red zone trip was smart and athletic. Plenty of defenders chase after a quarterback on a bootleg, only to see the pass get off anyway or thrown away. Lawrence grabbed the nearest arm of Brosmer and yanked him down toward the ground before the quarterback made a rookie mistake to try and toss the ball to the line of scrimmage to avoid a sack.

Jones was happy to collect the mistake and race the other way for a pick-six. Up 10-0, Seattle was never threatened again. Minnesota did not convert a 3rd down until there was about a minute left in the third quarter. Two plays later, Brosmer threw another interception to Coby Bryant.

Tariq Woolen got his first interception of the season and Jones got a second. He became the first player in Seahawks history to have two interceptions, one touchdown, and 12+ tackles in a game. His five interceptions on the season are the most for a Seahawks linebacker.

His presence on this team cannot be overstated. He is

everything you want in a leader. Smart. Passionate. Talented. Selfless. Seattle has won games without him, but make no mistake, they are a very different team when he is roaming the middle of this defense.

Love is expected to be back in the next week or so, and Jarran Reed should be back soon as well. Lawrence believes this defense has another level it can reach. He might be right. They are already as fearsome as any unit in the NFL. Ultimately, the fortunes of this team will rise and fall on their play.

The spending is on that side of the ball. The veterans are on that side of the ball. Macdonald and staff have a full year head start on Kubiak and the offense. All the fireworks on offense have been terrific. Don't let that fool you into believing the offense must excel for this team to win.

This defense has dismantled every offense they have faced outside of a Bucs team that was going against an unrecognizable crew that was missing Lawrence, Witherspoon, Woolen, and Love. That was the only game where Seattle allowed more than 24 points. Opponents are averaging 16.2 points per game when removing the Tampa Bay game.

Kubiak and Darnold need to be able to score 20+ points to reliably win with this defense. If they can score 25+, this team will be very tough to beat. A great special teams can help, and this was one of Jason Myers best games. He went 4-4 with two kicks of over 54 yards for the first time in his career.

Think back to the last two NFC Championship games the Seahawks hosted. The offense struggled in both. San Francisco led at halftime. Green Bay was running away with the game due to Wilson turnovers and ineffectiveness. It took a gritty ground game and a big-time explosive play on 4th down for Seattle to score enough points to beat the 49ers. It took some key turnovers and a special teams touchdown to help create enough opportunity for the offense to finish the job in overtime.

This Seahawks team has the elements it needs to be explosive downfield in the pass attack, with a defense and special teams that will always keep them in the game. Getting grittier in the run game is the most important step they can take between now and the playoffs, while also helping Darnold have more answers when teams send pressure.

The Rams team that had already started planning their victory parade dropped a game to the Carolina Panthers due to three costly Stafford turnovers. No team had been hotter or playing better football than the Rams. They were favored by 10 points. Carolina was playing without their best cornerback in Jaycee Horn. That Panthers team pounded the Rams defense on the ground and saw their defense make enough big plays to allow their quarterback to win the game on an explosive fourth down pass. We have seen this script before, both in terms of what it takes to beat a great team and how a great team can fall to a lesser opponent.

Seattle did not win a beauty pageant on Sunday. They did crush an opponent on their way to a 9-3 record and the best point differential in the NFL. That win combined with the Rams loss gives the Seahawks something that seemed unlikely just 24 hours earlier: control over their destiny in the NFC West. A 14-3 record will give Seattle a division title and a home game. That record, plus a loss by the Bears somewhere along the rest of the way (they play Green Bay twice, Detroit once, and the 49ers), would give Seattle the #1 overall seed and a first-round bye. Everything is on the table for Macdonald in his second season. He came to the northwest wanting to create a style of football that no opponent wanted to play against. That goal has been met. Bigger goals remain. ■

SEAHAWKS 37, FALCONS 9
December 7, 2025 • Atlanta, Georgia

LET THE GOOD TIMES ROLL

SEAHAWKS SMASH FALCONS FOR THIRD STRAIGHT WIN, IMPROVE TO 10-3

Open your favorite version of Madden and design a player. Drag the slider way over to the right for height, speed, leaping ability, strength, and work ethic, Keep dragging. When you hit the limit, send in a request to EA Sports asking them to set a higher limit for these skills. When they reply telling you that is not realistic, send them Nick Emmanwori's testing numbers and game film. A rookie class that will rank among the best in Seahawks history, may just add the franchise's first Defensive Rookie of the Year if Emmanwori continues to dazzle.

A slow-starting offensive game was made irrelevant by a collection of excellent performances on defense and special teams. Emmanwori was the headliner, making history as the first rookie in NFL history to have a blocked field goal, a sack, an interception, and two tackles for loss in one game. This was more of a festival, though, as Devon Witherspoon and Rashid Shaheed were putting on their own captivating shows.

Emmanwori was drafted, in part, to pair with Witherspoon and add almost endless flexibility to the Seahawks defense. Witherspoon had already established himself as one of the best nickel corners in football while making the Pro Bowl in each of his first two seasons. His ability to cover, defend the run, and rush the passer put him in exclusive company. Teams had started, however, to key on him as a blitzer, dulling his impact. Enter Emmanwori.

A player who would require a cheat code to unlock in a video game, fell out of the first round and into the Seahawks laps. He is capable of covering receivers, blowing up the run, and pressuring the passer. He is impossibly taller, heavier, stronger, and faster than Witherspoon while carrying out many of the same responsibilities.

That has allowed Witherspoon to play more boundary corner, while also making it far more difficult for an offense to slide protection one way or the other. The playful Witherspoon seems to relish torturing quarterbacks and offensive linemen before the snap, threatening to blitz before dropping into a coverage. When he does rush, he is more effective.

He entered this game with more pressures (nine) in eight games this season than he had in 17 games last year (eight). The terrorizing effect was on full display in this game as Witherspoon came on an early pressure to hit Kirk Cousins as he threw on a pass Julian Love expertly broke up. Later, he showed blitz, before reading a screen pass and tipping the ball up to himself for an interception, only his second in the NFL. He tipped another pass earlier that led to Emmanwori's first career interception. Oh, and he recovered a fumble as final brush stroke on his masterpiece.

Witherspoon is a player who often makes winning plays that are hard to quantify. He is the guy who makes the tackle in space for a 2-yard gain that would go for 40

Cornerback Devon Witherspoon and linebacker Ernest Jones IV team up to take down Falcons funning back Tyler Allgeier.

25
15

if he was not there. He slides into the throwing lane the quarterback wants to use, forcing the ball to be held for a second longer as the pass rush gets home. He helps put his teammates in position to succeed with pre-snap reads. He is your favorite player's, favorite player.

Both Emmanwori and Witherspoon missed considerable time earlier this year. Their net effect has increased as their time on the field as swelled and Mike Macdonald has learned how best to deploy them. That this was the first game all season that the Seahawks had every starter on defense available is remarkable. There are starters stacked on top of starters and playmakers at every level.

Consider that Tyrice Knight had two strip sacks a few weeks ago and is a backup right now. Or that the guy who took back the starting job, Ernest Jones IV, had two interceptions and a touchdown on his way to a Defensive Player of the Week award last week. DeMarcus Lawrence scored two touchdowns on those Knight strip sacks, forced a fumble last week, and was given credit for another forced fumble this week that might have actually come from Jarran Reed's club cast on his recovering hand and wrist. Ty Okada has been "phenomenal," in the words of Macdonald, and will most likely go back to special teams duty as Love takes back his starting role. Tariq Woolen and Josh Jobe are playing so well that the coaching staff cannot bring themselves to sit either of them.

Love was the original big nickel player for this defense, per Macdonald this week. That this team has at least four guys in Love, Emmanwori, Witherspoon, and Coby Bryant, who can play nickel and other positions, speaks to the confusion Macdonald wants to cause.

In a game where Atlanta largely refused risking straight dropbacks due to fear of the Seahawks pass rush, Seattle had to rely more on their secondary and linebackers to make plays on the perimeter and on screens. They mostly did a good job.

Bijan Robinson is a rare athlete in his own right, and he was doing his best to keep the Falcons close early. Seattle's streak of games without allowing a 100-yard rusher looked in jeopardy after he put up over 60 yards in the first half.

The Seahawks offense dragged out of the gates and had only three points until they got the ball with a little over a minute to go in the first half. Sam Darnold finally used his legs to scramble for yards and then made his best two throws of the day (to that point). One, to Shaheed, moved the team into field goal range. The other, was in rhythm to Barner for another five yards to make the job easier for Jason Myers, who has been locked in of late.

The kick tied the game at 6-6, with the Seahawks getting the ball back to start the second half. They didn't have it for long. Shaheed took the opening kickoff 100 yards to the house for a 13-6 lead. After a fumble recovery, Darnold marched the offense down the field for their first offensive touchdown of the day. At 20-6, the game felt over. Seattle was not done.

They would pile on 17 more points through a mixture of play-action pass and running plays that overwhelmed the Atlanta defense. Gone were the pressures that Seattle struggled with in the first half. Darnold played free and easy.

Klint Kubiak deserves a lot of praise for his adjustments and play calling in the second half. Many of the Darnold targets were to wide open receivers with room to run after the catch.

There was a glimpse of how this receiving corps can complement one another as Shaheed had his biggest day with 67 yards, Cooper Kupp had a nice run-after-catch and a touchdown, and Jaxon Smith-Njigba did his thing with nearly 100 yards and two TDs.

This season is one of the most unique in all the years I have watched the Seahawks play. Every number tells you this is either the best team in the NFL, or in the top two. They are unquestionably Super Bowl contenders. Yet, the hesitation to buy into this group is palpable.

Darnold is the primary throttle on fan enthusiasm. The performance against the Rams cannot be wiped away by any number of blowout wins against bad teams, especially when he continues to turn the ball over due to bad decisions. Holdout fans want to see Seattle beat a truly terrifying team.

The truth is, there are not many of them in the NFL this year. Los Angeles might be the only true powerhouse outside of Seattle. Even if the Seahawks beat them next week, many will still hold their breath until Darnold proves he will not be an impediment in the playoffs.

The flaw in that mindset, besides missing the joy of a fantastic season, is that you can pick any team other than the Rams and choose a variety of weaknesses that their fans know could end their season. The reason Seattle

Devon Witherspoon celebrates a fumble recovery as the Seahawks crested to a third straight win. Witherspoon also contributed with an interception and a key pass breakup.

and LA stand out the way they do is how good they are across the board.

It may ultimately be more about coaching than Darnold. Kubiak again decided to eschew the run on 3rd and short for a play-action pass that resulted in Darnold's interception. The coach's job is to put the players in the best position to succeed. Limiting dropbacks limits interceptions. That is not theory. It is math.

The Seahawks run game continues to show signs of life. Feed it. Let it flourish. Darnold will almost certainly continue to make questionable decisions and have turnovers. Jimmy Garoppolo made a Super Bowl in this offense. Jared Goff made a Super Bowl in this offense. Kubiak and Macdonald need to continue tinkering to find the best way to maximize the greatness Darnold brings, while minimizing the moments of mayhem.

Football games can be won in a variety of ways by a variety of players. Seattle not only is equipped to win in myriad of ways, but a roster full of Transformers who are capable of morphing from tank to jet to race car. This is truly great team full of fascinating people. Unleash this fanbase behind them, and there may be a #1 seed with a slate of home games in the playoffs ahead. Seattle will face quality opponents who will be fighting for playoffs and positioning. Their opponents will be facing the something far tougher. A storm is brewing in the PNW. Hit your local REI. Put on your favorite raincoat. Make your favorite throat-soothing drink. Your team needs you. Get off the sideline and strap up. ■

THE QUIET GENIUS

HOW THE MOST DOUBTED NFL OFFSEASON BECAME JOHN SCHNEIDER'S MASTERPIECE

DECEMBER 11, 2025

The room was overflowing. Players mixed with reporters, team staffers, and family members as they waited for confirmation of news they already knew. Pete Carroll strode onto the stage with the same pep that had made him a championship-winning coach and a beloved figure by all who crossed his path. His time as head coach and leader of football operations was ending. Tears flowed as he thanked his wife, Glenna, for her support through the years before politely answering questions. He closed by offering his support and a friendly warning to John Schneider, his longtime Seahawks partner, and the man tasked with following a legend:

"It has been 14 years that he's been sitting there waiting for his opportunity, and he deserves it. He's great at what he does, and now he's going to find out," Carroll paused for effect and grinned at Schneider as he reiterated, "You're gonna find out, big fella."

With that, the man who got most of the credit and blame for the past 14 years of Seahawks football, exited the stage and ended an era. Air cover, gone. Spotlight, on. Schneider became the final word on football operations for the first time in his career. He would be tasked with not only filling the shoes of one of the most popular figures in franchise history but turning around a football team that was going in the wrong direction.

A team that had made its mark with a historically dominant defense, was having trouble stopping anyone. The offensive and defensive lines were a mess. The roster had a number of aging and costly vets. Seattle had not won a playoff game in five years and had the 5th-longest conference championship drought in the NFC. Two years later, Seattle leads the NFL in point differential with a 10-3 record, and Schneider is the favorite to be named NFL Executive of the Year. This is the story of how it happened.

THE COACH

John Schneider had the notes ready for fourteen years.

From his early days in Green Bay alongside Mike Holmgren and Andy Reid, to his time in Kansas City with Marty Schottenheimer, Schneider had been quietly compiling a profile of the perfect head coach. When Pete Carroll departed, the expectation was that Schneider would finally open that notebook and make the safe play: hire old friend Dan Quinn or follow the NFL's current obsession and grab an offensive guru to nurture a quarterback.

But Schneider has never played it safe. This is the executive who drafted 5'10" quarterbacks when the league wanted height and helped build the Legion of Boom with oversized corners when the league wanted speed. Convention has never been a barrier to talent for John Schneider; usually, it's just noise he ignores.

So, while the Titans, Panthers, and Falcons rushed to interview Mike Macdonald in the early window—only to pass on him for offensive stability or familiar faces—Schneider waited.

He didn't view the delay as a disadvantage; he viewed it as due diligence. Seattle missed the early interview window partly to ensure the candidate met a broader cross-section of the organization, a process that required extensive diversity training for the staff.

Seahawks general manager John Schneider laid the foundations for Super Bowl success with key personnel decisions and a culture-defining sense of humility.

CONFERENCE
CHAMPIONS

"It spoke to John's humility," said Assistant GM Nolan Teasley. "He wanted to incorporate everybody... to ultimately make the best decision."

While Schneider waited, his network went to work. Titans executive Chad Brinker and Falcons GM Rich McKay signaled back a consistent message regarding Macdonald: *He crushed the interview.*

When the hiring window finally opened for playoff coaches, the Seahawks contingent—including owner Jody Allen—flew to Detroit first. The target was Lions OC Ben Johnson, the hottest name on the market. But after that meeting, the group knew they still had to see the young defensive coordinator from Baltimore.

It was a meeting that changed the franchise's trajectory.

The conversation with Macdonald didn't just go well; it was electric. Hours "felt like minutes." In Macdonald, Schneider didn't just find a coach; he found a partner who shared his vision. He bypassed the flashy offensive options and the familiar to hire a man who had never been a head coach before, and would become the league's youngest.

The gamble has paid off.

Macdonald is now the first coach in Seahawks history to win 10 games in each of his first two seasons. perhaps most impressive is the grit the team shows away from home: Macdonald is 13-2 on the road and has yet to drop a dreaded 10 AM kickoff, exorcising a demon that has haunted Seattle for decades.

While fellow 2024 hires like Dan Quinn and Jim Harbaugh found early success, Macdonald has elevated Seattle to a different tier. This season, his Seahawks dismantled Quinn's Commanders and Morris's Falcons by a combined score of 75-23.

Schneider may have waited fourteen years to make his first coaching hire, but looking at the standings today, it is clear: Macdonald was worth the wait.

THE CULTURE

For over a decade, the identity of the Seattle Seahawks was synonymous with noise. It was the brash swagger of the Legion of Boom, the relentless energy of Carroll, and a stadium that registered on seismographs. But as the franchise turned the page to a new era, the culture began to shift. The noise didn't disappear, but the frequency changed. The current Seahawks locker room is less about bravado and more about a quiet, lethal cohesion.

It is a culture that mirrors the man who has been there all along, operating in the background: Schneider.

Schneider's leadership style is antithetical to the ego-driven nature of the NFL. He is governed by a midwestern work ethic and a profound humility. "Plan. Communicate. Work. And then we are going to outwork people," Schneider says of his philosophy on the Finding Mastery podcast. "Nobody is smarter than anybody else. If you feel like you're smarter than anyone else, you and I are going to have a big problem working together."

This humility filters down from the front office to the field. Where the Carroll era was defined by loud, larger-than-life personalities, this roster—anchored by players like Jaxon Smith-Njigba, Leonard Williams, Sam Darnold, and Ernest Jones—carries a different demeanor. They are poised, soft-spoken, and intensely focused. They are a reflection of a GM who admits his own mistakes to interns to create a "calming effect," proving that while perfection is impossible, accountability is mandatory.

"We tell everyone in the whole operation, when you get in the car in the morning, what are you thinking about how to improve the organization?" Schneider explains. "And when you put your head on the pillow, how do you feel about what you did to help the organization today? And we care about you. It's a reciprocal thing."

To instill this reciprocal care in a new coaching regime, Schneider made a pivotal, subtle move this past offseason. He didn't issue a mandate; he offered a resource. He recommended that his new head coach, Macdonald, sit down with high-performance psychologist Michael Gervais.

"John had the ability to understand the appetite Coach Mike had, the competitive drive to get better, and he put a choice in front of him instead of forcing it on him," Gervais notes.

Macdonald, who had spent the postseason watching other franchises, had come to a realization: the teams that won in January were "tough and connected." He wanted that connection to run deep, crossing the traditional divides of offense, defense, and special teams. With the help of Gervais

Having identified a vulnerability in the Seahawks' roster, John Schneider opted to select North Dakota State guard Grey Zabel in the 2025 NFL Draft. Zabel, the 18th overall pick, quickly earned a starting role on the title-bound team.

SEAHAWKS
76
SEAHAWKS
NFL
50
76

and former Seahawk Steven Hauschka, Macdonald built a psychological framework to turn that desire into reality.

A key cornerstone of this plan was the "Walk and Talk."

Every Thursday, the team breaks into random groups of five—guys who might never otherwise speak—and takes a walk. They are given a topic, but the groundwork was laid weeks prior. "We asked the athletes to identify their purpose in life. We asked them to share experiences that made them themselves," Gervais explains. "And then so we extended that into the walk and talk... Coach Mike is basically creating space for people to know each other better."

The results were immediate and profound.

"Believe it or not, Michael [Dickson], our punter, we were on a walk and talk and I knew he was competitive, but I didn't realize he takes it to heart like he does," defensive tackle Jarran Reed recalls. "How much pride he takes in doing his job made me look at him in a different sort of way... It's been a minute since I've seen that in a locker room."

Leonard Williams echoes the sentiment, noting that understanding a teammate's "why"—seeing pictures of their families or hearing their struggles—changes the dynamic on the field. "If I see someone having a hard or tough day... I know his 'why' now, and how to talk to him and push him a little better."

This psychological investment is not just about feel-good vibes; it is a competitive safeguard. Gervais posits a simple theory: "When you know each other, you'll be more likely to have each other's back in a difficult moment, in a challenging moment. And what makes a great team is great teammates."

That theory was put to the ultimate test in Week 11.

Following a brutal loss to the Los Angeles Rams, in which quarterback Sam Darnold threw four interceptions, the critics were circling. In many locker rooms, fingers would have been pointed. Instead, linebacker Ernest Jones stepped to the podium and erected a wall around his quarterback.

"It's football, man. He is our quarterback and we got his back," Jones said, his voice steel. "If you have anything to say, quite frankly, fuck you."

It was a moment that proved the "Walk and Talks" were more than an exercise—they were armor. It was the "brotherhood" JSN speaks of, the "1000%" commitment that extends off the field and into the city.

Macdonald sees Schneider's influence in all of it. "He's kind of, you know, watering the plant to grow," the coach says. "I'm looking back at last year and I'm like, man... we're not even close. And so I'm looking back from John's perspective, I'm sure he saw the big thing."

The "big thing" is a culture of resilience, built not on volume, but on value. It is a testament to an executive who prefers to lead by example rather than decree. As Gervais observes, "John is in a really cool phase right now. You can feel John's imprint across the organization, and it really is like the hand that leaves the pond without a trace."

The ripples, however, are undeniable.

THE QUARTERBACK

In the NFL, finding a franchise quarterback is difficult. Knowing exactly when to get move on from one is nearly impossible.

The "perfect exit" is an art form: extract Pro Bowl production, sell high before the decline, secure trade assets, and immediately upgrade the position for cheaper. Even the infamous DeShaun Watson trade does not qualify as the Texans wandered the QB desert for two years before drafting C.J. Stroud. It is a sequence so difficult to execute that research suggests it has happened only four times in NFL history.

Schneider is responsible for two of them.

The first was the Russell Wilson trade, a move now widely regarded as one of the greatest heists in sports executive history. Schneider sold a declining asset for a historic haul, getting younger and more flexible while Denver footed the bill.

Then, he did it again.

Geno Smith had resurrected his career in Seattle, earning two Pro Bowl nods and outplaying Wilson's final Seahawks season. But when Smith demanded a contract north of $50 million with multi-year guarantees, Schneider didn't blink. He saw a 35-year-old quarterback at his ceiling. When Carroll returned to the NFL with the Las Vegas Raiders, Schneider seized the opportunity, shipping Smith to his former mentor for a third-round pick.

Macdonald had been steadfast that the Seahawks wanted Smith back. New offensive coordinator, Klint Kubiak, spoke effusively about Smith at his initial press conference. It would have been tempting for many GMs to bend in order to make life easier for the coaching staff.

Schneider had already been working on backup plans.

"He has a great like poise about him," Macdonald said. "It was just like, okay, we're going to pivot, and let's go. I think John deserves a lot of credit for like kind of setting the temperature for the whole thing."

That pivot was Sam Darnold.

To the rest of the league, Darnold was a "buyer beware" candidate—a 27-year-old free agent despite winning 14 games and throwing 35 touchdowns for Minnesota the prior year. The Vikings had moved on to their drafted rookie, leaving Darnold in limbo. Schneider saw an arbitrage opportunity: a quarterback in his prime who fit the direction of the offense, the culture, and commanded a lower price than Smith.

The results have been historic. Darnold is now just the second quarterback in NFL history to win 10+ games in consecutive seasons for different teams. The only other player to do it? Tom Brady.

Ironically, reports suggest it was Brady—now part of the Raiders' ownership group—who nixed signing Darnold in Vegas, preferring to trade for Smith instead. It was a costly miscalculation that Schneider happily exploited.

While questions remain about Darnold's postseason ceiling, the verdict on the process is undeniable. Schneider has upgraded the most important position in sports twice in four years by selling high and buying smart.

"Bill Walsh was big on saying there's a small percentage of people that have any clue what they're doing when they look at a quarterback," says former scout John Middlekauff. "I would say John's track record now... feels pretty good."

THE HATERS

MacGyver was a show in the 80s and 90s that featured the most resourceful hero of all time. He would take normal household items and use them to create a trap or defuse a bomb. MacGruber was developed by Will Forte, of *Saturday Night Live,* to poke fun at *MacGyver*. MacGruber would also use common items to try and defuse a bomb, except he was never successful, blowing up everything and everyone.

Schneider faced an offseason that was going to require him to leverage every resource at his disposal to handle a series of massive transitions. He had decisions to make on his quarterback, his most athletically gifted receiver, his perennially problematic offensive line, and support his head coach in bringing aboard a new offensive coordinator and new scheme. One wrong move, and everything blows up. It was a *MacGyver* or *MacGruber* offseason, and analysts almost universally predicted the worst.

Schneider came under heavy fire for his decision to trade both Smith and D.K. Metcalf. The ensuing choices to sign Darnold, fanned the flames. He was viewed as an inferior quarterback who would not have the same supporting cast or coaching that he had in Minnesota.

There was doubt outside Seattle that Jaxon Smith-Njigba could step into the primary receiver role, or even play outside of the slot. Many questioned whether the offensive line had been improved enough by just adding a rookie from a small school.

There was also skepticism about the addition of veteran defensive end DeMarcus Lawrence, who had missed most of last year with a foot injury and had contemplated retirement.

Vegas shared the skepticism. Seattle has a preseason over/under win total projection of 7.5 wins, behind teams like the Arizona Cardinals (8.5), Miami Dolphins (8.5), and Minnesota Vikings (8.5).

The critics were not only wrong on each count, but the degree to which Schneider proved to have the Midas touch was staggering.

OFFENSIVE LINE MAKEOVER

The Seahawks offensive line has been the butt of many jokes for over a decade. From 2015-2023, the Seahawks allowed 408 sacks, 3rd-most in the NFL, and a 7.9% sack rate, 2nd-highest in the NFL. Their coaching staff and front office have come under considerable fire for their lack of investment in the position, especially interior offensive line.

Mike Macdonald took over as coach in 2024, but the problems continued. Seattle ranked 24th in sack rate, adding another 50 sacks to their seemingly never-ending misery. Their starting center, Connor Williams, even retired over their bye week.

Macdonald fired their offensive coordinator, Ryan Grubb, after one season, citing philosophical differences that appeared to center around the lack of utilization of the run game and play-action. Kubiak was hired, and he brought veteran offensive line coach John Benton, along with Rick Dennison and Justin Outten.

Kubiak was clear this would be an outside zone running

team with counters off that, that included play-action and rollouts that moved the pocket.

Seattle went from 28th in run rate (37.2%) in 2024 to 1st in 2025 (51.1%). Their play-action rate rose from 29th (17.3%) last season to 10th (26.5%) through Week 12 in 2025. They also put heavy emphasis on under center snaps, seeing their under-center rate more than double (23.2% to 55.6%) from the previous season.

Schneider was steadfast that the solution to the problem was not just personnel. Scheme, coaching, and development were crucial.

He went hard after free agent guard Will Fries but lost out on him when he balked at taking a physical. That may have been a fortunate turn of events as it increased the priority of taking a guard in the draft, where they grabbed North Dakota State star, Grey Zabel.

Zabel was the first guard Seattle had used a Top 20 pick on since Hall of Famer Steve Hutchinson was taken 17th overall in the 2001 draft. He has become an immediate starter and the choice of some for Offensive Rookie of the Year.

The high-risk path of relying on young players has led to a dramatic turnaround. Seattle entered Week 14 as the most improved offensive line by ESPN's Pass Block and Run Block Win Rate metrics. Their sack rate has almost been cut in half from 8.3% to 4.5%.

DEFENSIVE GEMS IN FREE AGENCY

Lost in the uproar was the Seahawks resigning inside linebacker, Ernest Jones IV, to a three-year, $28.5M contract and defensive tackle, Jarran Reed, to a three-year, $22M deal. Those two moves ensured Seattle would return 10 of 11 starters from a defense that finished among the top five in a variety of measures over the final half of the 2024 season.

One of the challenges in the final years with Carroll had been a tendency to hold onto players and coaches too long. By contrast, Schneider's willingness to trade both starting inside linebackers he had signed in 2024 (Tyrel Dodson, Jerome Baker) before the season ended, dramatically accelerated the growth of Macdonald's defense.

Jones has been acquired in one of those deals and had quickly become a leader and core part of the defense. It also gave Jones a chance to get to know his coaches and teammates and be open to making it a long-term arrangement. Seattle would have gone into the offseason unsure of who would fit at one of the most important positions on Macdonald's defense had Schneider had any shred of ego about moving on from Dodson and Baker.

STELLAR DRAFT

Many of the critics also missed the draft capital that Schneider had acquired in trading Smith and Metcalf.

Seattle entered the draft with two picks in the 2nd round and two more in the 3rd round. That gave Schneider the flexibility move around the draft board and acquire two different players they would have been happy to take with their 1st round selection.

After picking Zabel, the team traded the 2nd round pick they received from the Steelers for Metcalf to help move up and draft athletic hybrid defender, Nick Emmanwori. This was a position Seattle tried to address the previous year with Rayshawn Jenkins, but the extra year of collaboration between the scouting department and the coaching staff allowed them to dial in their target this time.

Matt Berry, Seahawks VP of Player Acquisition, noticed the difference this offseason.

"We know exactly what a Mike Macdonald edge [player] looks like and what it does not," Berry said. "There is more specificity and less ambiguity. When you know what fits the role, it's easier to find those players and you can be more pointed in your acquisition."

The team got three more starters out of the draft, including tight end Elijah Arroyo, fullback Robbie Ouzts, and receiver Tory Horton. Horton was second among all rookies in touchdowns (6) after Week 9 before missing some time due to injury.

Former scout, John Middlekauff, who has worked with great GMs like Howie Roseman sees a direct tie between Schneider's continued willingness to get his hands dirty with scouting to the quality of the personnel decisions he has made.

"Most of these GMs now tend to be more like corporate CEOs," Middlekauff said. "Even guys that were football backgrounds, like John, they're in the office all the time, and they kind of get away from maybe their roots of going to schools and the scouting aspect. The amount of times over the last decades, that I have gotten selfies from my scouting buddies at a game with John Schneider watching Will Levis at Kentucky, or at the Oregon game, that is not normal. And no one's holding you to that."

DÉJÀ VU?

Carroll and Schneider led a historic collection of talent in shockingly short amount of time. They inherited one of the NFL's oldest rosters, bereft of talent, and turned it into a Super Bowl winner by their fourth year. Schneider was new to the role. Carroll was not.

After a decade of meandering through mediocrity, Seattle is rising once again. Schneider now plays the role of seasoned veteran. Macdonald is roughly the same age Schneider was when he started his first GM job here. At the core of it all is a vision and principles that reflect humility and hard work.

The connection between the two men is the bedrock for what has become one of the most talented, tough, and connected locker rooms in the NFL. Defying convention and skeptics, Schneider has guided the organization through a minefield and toward another sustained stretch of championship-caliber football.

It has not gone unnoticed.

"There is probably not a guy that is more consistently highly thought of in the NFL with peers than John Schneider," Middlekauff said. "People rave about how good he is at his job. And now it's like, the proof is in the pudding. I mean, just watch his team play"

On that emotional day in January, Pete Carroll offered a final, grinning warning to his successor: "You're gonna find out, big fella." And he was right. John Schneider did find out. He found out what it feels like when the "air cover" vanishes and the critics—from Vegas oddsmakers to national pundits—predict your collapse. He found out the weight of trading away his starting quarterback and the scrutiny of handing the keys to a rookie head coach.

But in navigating those minefields, Schneider found out something else. He discovered that a culture built on humility and connection can silence the noise. He found that his vision, executed in partnership with Mike Macdonald, could turn a rebuilding roster into a contender. Carroll warned him that he would find out how hard the job was. Schneider proved he was ready for the challenge. The rest of the league? They are the ones who are finding out. ■

SEAHAWKS 38, RAMS 37 (OT)
December 18, 2025 • Seattle, Washington

SHIFTING THE NARRATIVE

SEAHAWKS DISAPPOINT, DELIGHT IN STIRRING WIN OVER RIVAL RAMS

Lights flickered in the Northwest. A powerful wind swept across the state of Washington, threatening to add widespread power outages to a region already grappling with devastating floods. In the midst of this demonstration of nature's force, a football game took place.

The whole nation would watch as the two best teams in the NFL clashed under the lights of Lumen Field. Energy pulsed through the stadium in anticipation of this titanic rematch. There was hope. There was fear. What transpired over the next four hours was something even Mother Nature would appreciate, as unique as a snowflake. Hope flickered. Fears were realized. Perilously close to the darkest day of the year, another sort of Big Dark loomed in Seattle. But this was not a night for horror stories. Forty-eight men instead authored a fairy tale. A stadium that has been home to Beast Quakes and Fail Marys reminded everyone what magic feels like. The Seahawks are 12-3. The lights never went out. They just got brighter.

This was a night that rekindled lost love or started it anew. Strangers hugged. A region united in celebration. Kids discovered why mom and dad yell at the TV and wear weird costumes on Sunday. At the heart of this story is Sam Darnold.

Darnold is the everyman. His demeanor is reserved and impish. The wry grin when questioned hints of more substance behind the curtain than he chooses to reveal. He is Americana. His grandfather was the original "Marlboro Man." His father worked as a plumber. It was from these roots that the humble, crimson-haired quarterback grew. His football career has been a series of highs and lows. A former top pick, he failed repeatedly in his first NFL stop. His rise from the ashes last year in Minnesota came crashing down in two final games that cost him a job and millions in free agency.

Reborn in Seattle, Darnold was near the top of every MVP discussion before facing the Rams the first time. Disaster struck. His four-interception performance left the outside world dismissing him again. Few seemed to notice that he nearly helped win that game for his team even on his worst day.

The weeks that followed created a rift in the Seahawks fanbase. Seattle won every game. They were in position to accomplish things this franchise has not seen in over a decade. Yet, many fans were hesitant to hitch their hearts to a team with Darnold at the helm. He was too erratic. Better to keep your distance than risk being made a fool by believing something special was possible. It all culminated in this game.

Darnold helped author an opening drive touchdown with an explosive screen pass to Ken Walker III. The offense

Wide Receiver Rashid Shaheed runs downfield during a tense Week 16 matchup against the Rams. Shaheed's punt return for a touchdown provided the boost of energy the Seahawks needed.

SEAHAWKS
22

stalled for two drives, and then a great throw by Darnold was fumbled by Cooper Kupp as the team looked to be driving for at least a field goal before the half.

It was clear the coaches were trying to take some of the burden off his shoulders with a better run game and less risky throws. The plan was working, in the sense that Darnold had not put the ball in harm's way. Another explosive play from Walker after halftime put the Seahawks ahead 14-13. They were winning as a team.

The game ultimately required more of Darnold. He was not up to the task. Rams corner Josh Wallace abandoned his coverage responsibilities to jump a pass and nearly return the interception for a touchdown. Later, trailing by 16 points in the 4th quarter, Darnold was hammered by a Rams defender and threw the ball directly to a dropping defensive lineman for a second interception.

Seattle had a 3% chance to win the game, per NFL Next Gen Stats. That felt generous. Skeptical fans felt vindicated. Faithful fans were despondent. The questions were not going to be whether Darnold could recover from this performance, but whether the Seahawks could justify keeping him as a starter in years to come.

Newcomer Rashid Shaheed may have brought voodoo with him from New Orleans, as he helped bring the dead back to life for the second time in three games on special teams. His punt return for a touchdown gave Darnold a do-over at nearly the same spot where he threw his last pick. This time, he found Kupp for a two-point conversion, and the game was impossibly within one score with over eight minutes remaining.

Shaheed again sparked life with a 31-yard end-around that preceded a perfect parabola from Darnold to tight end A.J. Barner for a touchdown. It was his first touchdown pass in seven quarters.

The two-point try that followed was so bizarre, it already has been given a name. Darnold attempted to hit Zach Charbonnet on a screen, but the pass ricocheted off the helmet of a Rams defender and fell harmlessly to the ground in the end zone. Charbonnet casually strolled over to pick up the loose ball and give it to an official. Fairy dust must have fallen briefly instead of rain, as replays confirmed the pass went backwards, making it a fumble instead of an incomplete pass. Charbonnet making a clear recovery in the end zone meant Seattle had completed the most unlikely two-point conversion since, well, Russell Wilson tossed a ball into the atmosphere before it fell into the hands of Luke Willson in almost the exact same spot where Charbonnet recovered the fumble. Now dubbed The Zachwards Pass.

It was almost the perfect way to fuse the absurdity of improbable moments from the Seahawks' glorious past with the promise of this future. A baptism by silliness. Anger and despair were replaced with elation in a way that only sports seem to provide.

Darnold was not done. Tasked with bringing the team from behind once more after the defense surrendered a touchdown in overtime, Darnold had no margin for error. Seattle not only needed a touchdown, they needed a third two-point conversion to own the tiebreaker over the Rams and have a shot at the #1 overall seed in the NFC.

He found Jaxon Smith-Njigba on a beautiful throw and catch along the sideline before delivering maybe his best throw of the night to Kupp along the same sideline while a defender slammed into his chest. The ball was perfectly placed over the outstretched arms of one defender and settled into the arms of Kupp. A few plays later, Darnold would find Smith-Njigba again for a touchdown along the back end line.

It was fitting that the final play of the game was in Darnold's hands. The power of doubt is that all a doubter needs is a shred of evidence to feed their narrative. Even with all Darnold had done right to get the Seahawks to 11 wins and back to the point in this game where his team was in position to take control of the conference,

Despite early errors, Sam Darnold was able to deliver against the Rams. Darnold found Jaxon Smith-Njigba for a crucial touchdown in overtime, then connected with Eric Saubert for the two-point conversion.

SEAHAWKS
SEAHAWKS
14
12

FORBES JR
1
SEAHAWKS
81
88

any play that resulted in failure would have been used like a sledgehammer to pound him back into the pigeonhole they want him in.

Patiently, Darnold went through his progressions. His feet and shoulders moved in unison as he clicked through his first, second, and third read. All were covered. Finally, his fourth read, tight end Eric Saubert, released from a block and found himself wide open for a winning conversion that will be talked about for generations.

There is poetry in how this game played out. Darnold's errors will likely be remembered more than his contributions to the tapestry of great plays across the team that resulted in the win. He will forever face doubters, waiting to pounce and prove themselves right. Darnold operates outside the purview of doubt. His greatest superpower is his ability to let go of his mistakes in pursuit of the next great play. It has helped him revive a career that was left for dead and lead two different franchises to the playoffs in back-to-back seasons. He has a chance to lead both teams to 14 wins, which would be the first time a QB has done that in consecutive seasons since Tom Brady in 2003 and 2004.

Darnold is not the face of this team. This team remains largely faceless. He is the lightning rod. Storms will continue to swirl. Opponents are beginning to realize that while Darnold can thrive in spite of repeated strikes, they may not survive what comes next. ■

Tight end Eric Saubert celebrates after receiving Sam Darnold's pass for a game-winning two-point conversion.

SEAHAWKS 13, 49ERS 3
January 3, 2026 • Santa Clara, California

A CUT ABOVE

SEAHAWKS BIGGER, FASTER, SMARTER, BETTER AS TOP SEED

The lobby was quiet. Rain was falling outside, as if Mother Nature wanted the Bay Area to know who was coming to town. To the left was a lonely hotel employee behind a dimly lit front desk. To the right, the hotel bar and restaurant were sprinkled with Seahawks staff, coaches, and players. Two players, Jake Bobo and Jaxon Smith-Njigba, sat in a lounge area, focused intently on the chess board between them. One would make a move. The other would counter. Bobo ultimately wound up the victor, and welcomed in his next opponent, Drake Thomas. Later, Jalen Sundell and Mason Richman sat down to play. It had the feel of a family vacation. No nerves. No loud music. As they have been so many times this season, the Seahawks were at home even when on the road. Mike Macdonald has had his team playing chess all season while the rest of the NFL is playing checkers. Never was that more clear than during a 13-3 dismantling of the rival 49ers in Santa Clara.

It is often difficult to recognize and cherish something as truly special in the moment. This Seahawks team has mixed pleasure with pain all season. Their quarterback went from the MVP conversation to meme material. Their right guard was mercilessly chided for lowlights and called the worst player in the NFL. The linebacker room was considered understocked and undersized. Their freakishly athletic corner was crushed for early season errors. One of their running backs was accused of losing a step, while the other was accused of never having one to begin with.

The Seahawks were rude to their hosts on Saturday night as they stepped all over the 49ers. Ken Walker III and Zach Charbonnet took turns hammering a weak San Francisco defense. The offensive line, even without their starting left tackle and with a hobbled backup, pushed the 49ers around from the opening snap to the final play. Sam Darnold made good decisions all evening, using his legs when it made sense, and checking the ball down.

Seattle ran the ball at will, inside and outside, with either running back and to either side. They did not turn the ball over, and possessed the ball for over 37 minutes, limiting their opponent to just eight drives. Jaxon Smith-Njigba sprinkled in some of his magic, and Cooper Kupp made some crucial catches on 3rd down. The scoreboard did not reflect how efficiently Seattle played. Their 40.1 yards per drive was their highest since their blowout against the Commanders (41.8 yds/drive).

I have talked about how the Seahawks offense was going through a reverse metamorphosis. They were the beautiful butterfly, electrifying fans with the explosive passing attack while their running game was largely nonexistent. A combination of opponent adjustments and Seahawks coaches' foresight led them down a path of turn-

Ken Walker III was the game's leading rusher against San Francisco, totaling 97 yards on 16 carries.

SEAHAWKS
9

ing this into a physical running team.

San Francisco defensive coordinator, Robert Saleh, was committed to limiting explosive plays. That left a light box for the Seahawks to run against. It felt like a 1990s Mike Tyson fight with an early knockout. A picture-perfect opening drive inexplicably ended with a decision to pass the ball from the 1-yard line (STOP DOING THAT SEAHAWKS COACHES) that resulted in a sack, and eventually a turnover on downs. No matter. Seattle bludgeoned them again on the next drive, with Charbonnet breaking a big run for the lone touchdown in the game.

Grey Zabel, Anthony Bradford, and Jalen Sundell were considered the biggest question marks on the offensive line heading into the season. They dominated in this game. Bradford has been a lightning rod for critics all season. The reality is he has some very poor snaps, but what people fail to understand is that his dominant and neutral snaps far outnumber his lowlights. Zabel was brilliant in this one, working out in space and serving breakfast for dinner with 49er pancakes all over the field. Sundell might have played his best game as a pro.

These former college roommates sat shoulder-to-shoulder on folding chairs in front of their lockers with cigars dangling from their grinning mouths in a raucous postgame locker room. Sundell joked about how it felt like yesterday that he was teaching Zabel how to do laundry. Zabel reflected on how surreal the experience was to share with his friend. He planned on having a bunch of guys from the team over to his place on Sunday to watch football and drink Busch Lights.

Seattle took the riskier road by only adding a rookie to an already young offensive line this offseason. There are seven players on the line who are either in their first or second season in the NFL. The upside of the path they chose is this group has the potential to grow and stay together for years to come.

That group helped pave the way to the third straight game of over 160 yards rushing. Seattle has not accomplished that feat since 2021. It might be exactly the late-breaking growth they need to frustrate opponents in the playoffs. The Seahawks are 4th in EPA/rush over the last three games. That is quite the glow-up from a team that trotted out one of the least efficient run games in football for the first nine weeks of the season.

A team that can run the ball, limit turnovers and opponent possessions, and play elite defense, is a team that can win a Super Bowl.

Leonard Williams, Ernest Jones IV, and crew put on some kind of show for the world to see. This was the defensive equivalent of Marshawn Lynch grabbing his crotch as he crossed the goal line on the Beast Quake run. As Lynch used to say, you've got to stamp a special play. This defense put a stamp on a special season.

No offense was hotter coming into this game than the 49ers. Brock Purdy had scored five touchdowns in each of his last two games. He was prancing around the field like the game was too easy for him. He was barely able to walk off the field after this one.

Seattle's defense was everywhere. Teams strive to be a step ahead of their opponents. Macdonald had this Dark Side with M.O.B ties crew ten steps ahead of anything and everything Kyle Shanahan threw his way. Christian McCaffrey had been back to his Offensive Player of the Year level the previous two weeks, with over 140 scrimmage yards and a collection of touchdowns. Seattle held him to 57 scrimmage yards, no touchdowns, and a lot of bruises.

There was a point in the game where McCaffrey smacked his own helmet as he entered the 49ers huddle during a commercial break, as if to psych himself up to run through someone's face. Sure enough, he got the chance on the next play and took the handoff, determined to blow a hole in the Seahawks defense. Like the riders on horseback, carrying torches, as they hurdled toward the white walkers in Game of Thrones, his light was snuffed out.

Leonard Williams, Byron Murphy, Jarran Reed and everyone else who took the field for Seattle, reset the line of scrimmage over and over again. They bullied San Francisco in a way few Seahawks teams ever have.

Leonard Williams (top) and Derick Hall take down 49ers quarterback Brock Purdy. The Seahawks sacked Purdy three times in the win.

PURDY
13
HALL
58

It was a performance that stirred flashbacks of the Legion of Boom. More than that, it was a performance that signaled it was time to stop comparing this group to the past. Legacies will be written later. Right now, they are an impossible puzzle to solve. They are a Rubik's Cube covered in spikes and razor blades.

There is no question this team is led by their defense. And so it should be with Macdonald at the helm. Not only are they ultra-talented, but they are equipped with more veterans, more time in the system, and more vocal leaders. It is easy to forget this is Klint Kubiak's first year installing his offense, and most of the players on that side of the ball are young. There is reason to think they will continue to grow in year two the way this defense has.

Being led by an elite defense and a strong running game with a "good enough" quarterback was a championship formula for the Eagles last season. Seattle may not boast that running game, but their defense might be better.

Macdonald put the rest of the division on notice. The number of franchise records that fell in just his second season as head coach has Ravens fans crying into their morning coffee. I have seen the fraternity of offensive coaches at the league meeting during the offseason. They hang out like frat brothers, trading tales of their schematic brilliance. Macdonald is the growing shadow that lurks in their minds, of dark times and embarrassing results.

A lasting difference between Macdonald and guys like Sean McVay and Kyle Shanahan is his humility. He will stay grounded, even as his reputation elevates. He will look for the next way to improve and never seek the spotlight. His vision was to create a style of football that nobody else wants to play. He has done that in just his second season and will only get better as a coach.

Now he gets his first taste of postseason football as the man in charge. His defense and offense just put together arguably the most physically dominant performance of the season. They get two weeks to rest until their next game. Charles Cross will be back. Coby Bryant will return. Elijah Arroyo may join them. What may be most terrifying to the rest of the NFL is that Macdonald and his coaching staff get two weeks to self-scout and dissect opponent game film as well.

He is 2-0 coming off a bye week in his first two seasons. Seattle beat the 49ers in San Francisco last year after the bye and blew the doors off the Commanders after the bye this year. This is not just a defense-led team, but a defensive line-led team. Those guys tend to wear down over the course of a season more than most. The extra rest is going to be huge for guys like Williams and Reed and Murphy. Their level of dominance will be a determining factor in a Super Bowl run. Seattle does not lose when those guys eat.

Ironically, one of the most important areas of focus might be how to play their best football with the crowd noise at Lumen Field. The Rams took advantage of numerous communication breakdowns that players attributed, in part, to crowd noise. They do not want fans to get quieter. They do want to find a way to eliminate those errors.

These are 1-seed types of problems to have. For the first time since 2014, Seattle has a bye and home-field throughout the NFC portion of the playoffs. Win two games at home, and they take a short trip back down to the Bay for a chance to win a ring on their rival's home field. Sweet dreams are made of this.

Seattle will play its first divisional round playoff game since 2019. It will be their first home divisional round game since 2014. They have never lost a divisional round game at home. They have never lost an NFC Championship game at home. This team has done their part. Now it is time for Seahawks fans to bring their best.

That quiet hotel lobby is now empty. The chess pieces have been moved, the checkmate delivered, and the board resets in Seattle. The road to the Super Bowl goes through Lumen Field, where silence goes to die. The 12s have been waiting for a team worthy of their loudest roar. They finally have one. ■

Mike Macdonald and the Seahawks finished the regular season as the NFC's top seed, earning a bye and home-field throughout the NFC playoffs.

SONY
SONY
SONY
MIKE
MACDONALD

NFC PLAYOFFS

Best Mobile Network in the Game.
T Mobile
Now the Best Mobile Network in America.
T Mobile
DELTA
ticketmaster
DELTA SKY360°CLUB
DELTA SKY360°CLUB

NFC DIVISIONAL ROUND
SEAHAWKS 41, 49ERS 6
January 17, 2026 • Seattle, Washington

COOKING AT HOME

SEAHAWKS BURY 49ERS, EYE RAMS

The setting met the moment. Mike Macdonald talks about "chasing edges" in regard to all aspects of his football team. One edge they had yet to unlock was the multiplying force of Lumen Field.

Yes, the Seahawks finished the regular season 6-2 at home. Yes, their last home game had been a miraculous win against their toughest opponent in overtime. The case could be made, though, that the Seahawks were losing an edge when playing at home due to some errors on defense that helped lead to 37 points for the Rams in that game. Not on Saturday. Not against the zombie 49ers. Home field advantage was fully restored as part of a joyous, gory, 41-6 dismembering of their bitter division rival. Good thing, as Seattle will need every edge they can muster to beat the Rams next week and return to the Super Bowl.

Much has been made of the invasion of opposing fans into Lumen Field in recent years. I wrote extensively on the topic after doing research into the complexity underlying the problem. Most of the problems are going to be difficult to address. One challenge that can be overcome is exerting more control over who seats are sold to. Progress has been made on two fronts on that issue. The Seahawks have exerted some pressure to sell tickets to friends and family or risk losing their season tickets in the future. I have created HBTix.com to give sellers a way to better understand who is buying your tickets. Both approaches seemed to have helped limit the number of 49ers fans in the stands for this game.

This is not meant as a victory lap or a humble brag hoping for recognition. All I care about is the Seahawks winning every damn game possible, especially at home.

Consider this a progress report. We are taking back our house. It was buzzing in there Saturday night. The crowd was in their seats well before kickoff. Red jerseys were few and far between. I had become accustomed to some opposing fan being within a few seats of me at big games. There were none anywhere close to me at this game. It made the experience so much more communal, so much more enjoyable, even before Rashid Shaheed sent a lightning bolt through the stadium.

Fans were not just there in larger numbers, they were there with the intention to work. Screaming started when the 49ers were in their huddle instead of waiting for them to reach the line of scrimmage. That has not really happened much since 2005 when the crowd advantage tortured the NY Giants into countless false starts. Fans came to lift their team. I felt it. Players felt it.

Even as Brock Purdy ran a marathon behind the line of scrimmage, and made some discouraging, improbable, completions, the crowd sustained their energy

Zach Charbonnet carries the football during the Seahawks' divisional round win over the 49ers. Seattle rushers combined for 175 yards on 33 carries.

26
SEAHAWKS
26

Ken Walker III celebrates in the end zone after scoring one of his three touchdowns in the victory over San Francisco.

MUSTAPHA

and intent. This felt like a family reunion (with relatives you're happy to see).

The defense did their part, limiting the 49ers to just 6 points and avoiding some of the communication errors that plagued them against the Rams. This was a unique situation that allowed a bit of an apples-to-apples comparison of how the defense would perform against the same opponent on the road versus at home in back-to-back games.

The 49ers may have doubled their scoring output from three points to six points, but that required a 56-yard field goal to scrape over the upright. They never even entered the red zone. That was just the third time in Kyle Shanahan's tenure that his offense failed to reach the red zone. One of those games was in torrential rain last season against the Rams, where both offenses struggled in the elements. There was nothing but clear skies in Seattle.

This is not conclusive evidence that the Seahawks have addressed their challenges of playing defense with a loud crowd, but it is certainly a good sign.

Opponents need some sort of edge against this defense because they are choking the life out of teams. They are allowing 6.3 points per game and 182 yards per game over their last three games. Over their last seven games, which includes the 37 points from the Rams, they are allowing just 11.6 points per game. Remove the Rams game, and it's 7.3 points per game.

All the focus on the less explosive Seahawks offense caused many to miss the already elite defense getting better. You may hear about the Texans defense and the Broncos defense. None of them have been doing what Seattle has done.

They are defending well at all levels. Coverage is great. Run defense is moving toward historically good. Pass rush has been good, even if not dominating. They have held three straight teams (all playoff participants) to 128 or fewer passing yards and -0.59 EPA/pass or lower.

Ricky Pearsall played in this game. At least, that's the rumor. He finished with zero catches and zero yards. Jauan Jennings boasted about wanting to face the Seahawks last week. He had two catches for 23 yards, and a drop forced by Tariq Woolen.

Christian McCaffrey tortured the vaunted Vic Fangio Eagles defense. He was held to 35 yards rushing and 39 yards receiving. It was suffocating. It was glorious.

As good as the defense was, the special teams deserves the spotlight. Jay Harbaugh, once again, found a weakness in his opponent and exploited it. Patrick O'Connell confirmed in the postgame locker room that Harbaugh had the Seahawks start with a single returner back on kickoff and 10 men upfield. They had not run that formation much, or maybe at all.

It worked.

Shaheed took the opening kick back for a touchdown, avoiding the cheap shot tripping attempt by the 49ers kicker. The game was over at the point, even if nobody knew it. The 49ers were incapable of scoring even 7 points in this one.

Harbaugh has done this repeatedly with punt blocks, kick blocks, returns and even a kickoff touchdown recovery way back in Week 2 against the Steelers. He has been a central part of the Seahawks becoming this 15-win powerhouse.

Who knows how the game would have gone if the Seahawks offense took the field first. Maybe they would have scored as well. Maybe they would have struggled early, and San Francisco would have gained confidence. We will never know. What we do know is the Seahawks special teams are a weapon few teams have in their arsenal.

Once the offense did finally take the field, they put together a quality drive that stalled at the 49ers 13-yard line but did result in points. They scored on their first two possessions, and three of four in the first half. They wound up scoring on 6 of their first seven possessions.

They did it without needing to rely on Sam Darnold's arm thanks to a run game that has emerged as one of the best in football. Seattle has rushed for over 160 yards in four straight games. The 49ers were desperate to stop the run game after yielding 180 yards in Week 18. They stacked the box over 44% of the time, massively above their season average. It didn't matter.

Seattle run over, around, and through their defense for another 175 yards. Ken Walker III looked like the dynamic weapon I have believed him to be since touting him as an Offensive Player of the Year candidate in training camp. Walker attacked the line of scrimmage with an aggression we have not seen in his NFL tenure. He hit holes, found weak spots, and broke tackles all night. Every time he took a handoff, it felt like he was a threat to go the distance.

Some credit goes to run game coordinator, Justin Outten, who took over the running back room when Kennedy Polamalu left the team a few weeks back. Both Walker and Charbonnet appear to be playing their best football since that change. Robbie Ouzts also seems to have taken a step forward. It is probably not a coincidence that Eric Saubert returned from injury to help with the blocking.

Whatever the reason, Seattle has now found a threatening run game that was simply not part of their repertoire earlier in the season. It was just a few weeks ago that Macdonald said, "It's getting pretty late to figure it out." Better late than never.

That, combined with an also improved screen game, has given the Seahawks offense enough variety to challenge defenses who have committed to slowing down Jaxon Smith-Njigba and the explosive passing game. I was hoping to see that return a bit more in this game, knowing San Francisco would be more focused on stopping the run, but it did not.

There was a deep shot to Shaheed that fans have been clamoring for, but it was not close to complete. Still, the pass game had some nice moments. The touchdown pass to JSN was gorgeous. Multiple completions to Cooper Kupp were critical to sustaining drives. The run game allowed Darnold to carry less weight with his injured oblique.

Drew Lock did get to play, but not for the reasons so many were worried about. It is rare to blowout a playoff opponent so bad that you can insert your backup QB with plenty of time left to play. It is even more rare to do it against a divisional opponent that won 13 games and ousted the Super Bowl champs a week prior.

That is who this team is. They are capable of more.

The Rams scraped by the Bears in overtime a day after the Seahawks took care of business. They played an overtime game on the road and will have one fewer rest day than Seattle. Maybe that will matter.

What is crystal clear is that this will be an absolute dogfight on Sunday. Forget about how good the Seahawks have looked lately and how middling the Rams have been. These are the two best teams in football. They have elite players, elite coaches, and are brimming with confidence.

This is very reminiscent of the 2013 NFC Championship between the Seahawks and 49ers. The past did not matter in that game. Both teams traded haymakers. Seattle trailed in that game. They fumbled on the first play. They needed a 4th down touchdown pass and a fingertip pass breakup in the endzone to come away with the win despite being the most talented team in franchise history.

They were better than the 2014 Green Bay Packers, but they had to overcome five turnovers to pull off the most unlikely playoff win ever.

These games are not easy. There is no Jarrett Stidham in this game. Seattle will have to play their best game of the season to make it to the Super Bowl.

They enter with the most complete team in the sport, a rejuvenated home field, and new weaponry. The Seahawks have earned the right to compete in this game. They will approach it with the same process and focus they have attacked every opportunity. Edges have not just been chased and they have been secured. The Rams are about to find out just how sharp those edges have become. ■

NFC CHAMPIONSHIP

SEAHAWKS 31, RAMS 27

January 25, 2026 • Seattle, Washington

SPECTACULAR SAM MAKES SEATTLE SUPER

SAM DARNOLD AND SEAHAWKS CAPTURE THRILLER OVER RAMS, RETURN TO SUPER BOWL

The last time the Seahawks punched their ticket to the Super Bowl, it was with a brash band of brothers who took note of every slight, every doubt. They were 5th-round picks and undrafted free agents who had been passed over but rarely passed on. They were young and smart and terrifying for opponents.

This new crew shares the youth and intelligence and brotherhood, but their defining characteristic may be what differentiates them from the iconic Legion of Boom. Michael Strahan posed a question that would have been catnip for the LOB. "Coming into the season, you were an afterthought to the Rams and the 49ers. How does it feel to go through both of those teams to go to the Super Bowl?" Standing on a stage in the middle of a euphoric Lumen Field, head coach Mike Macdonald responded genuinely and defiantly, "We did not care."

The man who resists every attempt to add meaning or narrative to what his team is doing, captured the essence of this group in a phrase so efficient, Hemingway would be jealous. Make no mistake, this team is overflowing with stories worth telling, but their dedication to the game and each other is what sets them apart. Mission over bullshit. One more game to complete the mission.

This was not a revenge story. It was a love story. Sam Darnold has enough bulletin board material to occupy every bulletin board in the country. The grandson of the Marlboro Man could have burned every doubter after a heroic postseason performance, and nobody would have faulted him for it. That is not who he is, and not how this team operates.

Rewind 10 weeks. Darnold walked off a much smaller stage in the bowels of SoFi Stadium after pouring rocket fuel on the negative narratives burning throughout his career with a four-interception game. Ernest Jones IV made his way down a long hall to take the stage after Darnold. The two had to squeeze by each other in the narrow corridor, and Jones made a point to make eye contact with his quarterback and say, "I got you."

Jones climbed behind the podium and had a message that seemed directed outside the locker room but was very much for every one of his brothers in it.

"Man, Sam's been balling," Jones said. "If we want to try to define Sam by this game, man, Sam's had us in every fucking game. So for him to sit there and say, 'Oh, that's my fault,' no, it's not. There were plays that defensively we could have made, there were opportunities where we

Sam Darnold rolls out to pass against the Rams. Darnold passed for 346 yards and three touchdowns as the Seahawks advanced to the Super Bowl.

SEAHAWKS
14

could have got better stops. It's football, man. He's our quarterback, we've got his back, and if you've got anything to say, quite frankly, fuck you."

The Seahawks have not lost since Jones delivered those words. There is no way to prove Darnold would have fallen short of the flawless performance he put together to win the NFC Championship if Jones had chosen different words or had different feelings. Yet, we have seen numerous teams loaded with talent crumble under the weight of ego and finger pointing. This is not one of those teams.

This team rallied behind their embattled quarterback, and he repaid them by outdueling the MVP.

That cross-team cohesion was born out of a deliberate set of decisions by Macdonald to invest in the connection as much as execution. He saw that the teams that went furthest in the playoffs were the ones who shared a bond beyond the jersey they wore. He took the advice of John Schneider to work with sports performance psychologist, Michael Gervais and his associate Stephen Hauschka. They made every Thursday a day to foster that connection with walk-and-talks that paired players from different parts of the team. They intentionally mixed up the locker assignments so players on offense were intermingled with players on defense and special teams.

Macdonald and Schneider were intentional about who they brought in, and who they let go. Their draft was full of talent and low ego young men with charisma that infused the team with fresh energy. Kids games, like shadow boxing, broke out across the roster and persisted throughout the season.

This team loves one another. Even when one of them makes a foolish and selfish decision, like Tariq Woolen did when he chose to face his opponent's sideline instead of his teammates, they love each other.

There has been doubt about this team, this coach, and players ranging from Darnold to Woolen to Anthony Bradford to Cooper Kupp to Abe Lucas to Drake Thomas and on down the line. That doubt has come from outside national pundits and Seahawks fans. Had they been wired to make this run fueled by doubt, there was a plentiful and renewable supply.

What makes them the favorite to win this franchise's second Lombardi Trophy, and perhaps more in the future, is the detachment from doubt and hate. They are a team of ultra-talented individuals who are impervious the ups and downs of external perspectives. Others choose the roller coaster. They choose the light rail.

It is not always flashy, but it is dependable and sturdy.

This game required every bit of what they have to offer. The Rams offense was arguably the best unit in football this season. They proved that by beating up on the Seahawks defense twice. Seattle proved they were the better team by beating the Rams twice.

Matthew Stafford was every bit the MVP in this one. He had the determination and precision of The Terminator. Seattle could not shake him or contain him. His decision-making was exquisite. Some of the throws he made were obscene.

Maybe he was aided by Seahawks secondary players falling a few times. More likely, players were falling because they were getting put in bad positions by outstanding opponents.

Devon Witherspoon was having one of his worst games as a pro. He wrote an ending that changed his story. Stops on 3rd and 4th down wound up being enough for his team to punch their ticket to the title game.

The drive that followed was one of the best scoreless drives you will ever witness. It was fitting that the offense would be asked to start from their own 6-yard line in the same endzone that tortured them multiple times this season. There had been strip sack touchdowns and bad snaps and other miserable moments when backed up earlier in the year. Not this time. Not when facing the team that had forced six turnovers against this offense.

Ken Walker III started with a physical 4-yard run to provide some breathing room and start the clock ticking. Most people expected another run on second down. Klint Kubiak had other ideas. Knowing that his most advantageous passing situations were going to be on second down

Seahawks guard Anthony Bradford lead blocks ahead of running back George Holani during the NFC Championship win over the 49ers.

75
36
SEAHAWKS
75

14

when the Rams were needing to sell out against the run, he dialed up a high percentage pass play to Walker, who turned it into a 15-yard gain.

Back to Walker for three yards on the ground made it 2nd and 7 at the 28-yard line with 3:31 to go. Kubiak again eschewed the conservative call and went for a pass. Darnold could not connect with Rashid Shaheed, who clearly was contacted before the ball arrived without a flag being thrown. Clock stopped. Third and long.

Good thing the Seahawks have become good at converting 3rd and long.

Kubiak made a nice call, but the work from Darnold and Kupp was even better. In an absolutely need-it moment, Kupp got just enough to move the chains. If that doesn't happen, you are punting back to Stafford with over three minutes remaining.

Stuffed for no gain on the next play, Kubiak again went to the air and found Jaxon Smith-Njigba for another high percentage short throw that turned into another first down.

Each one of these decisions are magnified by a thousand in these moments. Every single minute poured into this season by everyone in the VMAC had brought the team to the precipice of a Super Bowl. Many people would crumble under that pressure. This franchise knows better than any how calling a pass when a run is the conventional wisdom can be scarring.

Kubiak's savvy and courage had brought the team to the Seattle 49-yard line with three minutes remaining. Another run by Walker and then another pass from Kubiak's playbook. This one fell incomplete, but the refs finally threw a flag on the Rams for holding. First down at the Rams 48-yard line with 2:12 to go.

Walker pushed the pile for 6 big yards on first down to get to the two-minute warning. The rest of the drive did not go as well, as the team had to punt, but the damage had been done. The Rams got the ball at their own 7-yard line with 25 seconds to go and no timeouts.

Sam Darnold throws one of his 36 pass attempts in the NFC Championship game.

Seattle moved the ball 49 yards and took 4 minutes and 29 seconds off the clock. They changed the field position from their 6-yard line to the Rams 7-yard line. The combination of Witherspoon's redemption and Kubiak's daring ultimately ended the Rams season.

They continued to be petulant losers after the final whistle, but it would be a betrayal of who this Seahawks team is to dwell on the ugliness of haters.

As Macdonald said, they do not care. It is ironic. Macdonald and Jones managed to demonstrate what they do care deeply about while emphasizing what they do not. They care about winning. They care about their standards. They care about each other. Bullshit never had a chance against this MOB. The Seahawk are super once again. ■

Above: Seahawks chair Jody Allen celebrates Seattle's NFC Championship victory. Opposite: Jaxon Smith-Njigba's touchdown catch in the second quarter gave the Seahawks a 17-13 lead going into halftime.

The celebration was on as Lumen Field remained packed in the aftermath of the Seahawks winning the NFC Championship.

TOYOTA
NFC CHAMPIONS
SEAHAWKS
SEA
MITSUBISHI ELECTRIC
HOME
FIELD

NATIONAL FOOTBALL
NFL